The People's Friend

2020 Annual

St Kilda, Outer Hebrides

THE archipelago of Hirta, Dun, Soay and Boreray is only a little over three square miles in total, and sits way out into the bleak Atlantic Ocean, 110 miles from the Scottish mainland. Yet it was inhabited for nearly four thousand years.

Battered by some of the strongest winds and highest waves in Europe, a community of hardy crofters eked out a living from sheep and seabirds. Eventually, outside pressures led the final 36 islanders to request evacuation to the mainland in 1930.

Since then, the islands have been the site of extensive scientific study – there are nearly a million seabirds here during the breeding season.

The remote location also means that several species have evolved separately from their fellows elsewhere; the islands are home to a unique wren, for example, and a mouse that is twice the size of a British field mouse!

The islands are owned by the National Trust for Scotland and are a UNESCO World Heritage Site. ■

Contents

Dear Readers . . .

It is with great pleasure that I welcome you to "The People's Friend" Annual 2020. With 25 brand-new short stories written by some of your favourite "Friend" authors and illustrated beautifully by our talented artists, all 176 pages are packed with great reading to keep you entertained the whole year through.

We have seasonal poems sure to uplift and enchant you, 10 fabulous watercolour paintings from J. Campbell Kerr and some fascinating highlights from the Olympic Games through the years.

I do hope you enjoy this year's Annual as much as we enjoyed creating it!

Angela

Angela Gilchrist, Editor

Complete Stories

6 For Auld Lang Syne
by Jean Cullop

14 Wise Words
by Moira Gee

20 A Precious Gift
by Jan Snook

26 A Life In Rhyme
by Natalie Kleinman

32 Hidden Treasure
by Samantha Tonge

40 A Boys' Day Out
by Jan Snook

48 Old School
by Donald Lightwood

54 The Whole Picture
by Annie Harris

61 For Tina
by Pamela Wray

68 London Calling
by Maggie Cobbett

76 A Lesson Learned
by Pamela Ormondroyd

86 The Corncochle Tree
by Moira Gee

94 Market Day
by Natalie Kleinman

100 Cheery And Bubbly
by Donald Lightwood

105 A Fairy Godmother
by Alyson Hilbourne

110 Ruby's Garden
by Sylvie Hall

116 Meet Me At The Bridge
by Christine Bryant

121 Pumpkin Magic
by Annie Harris

128 The Apple Dream
by Em Barnard

136 Useful Work
by Alison Carter

142 Welcome Home
by Teresa Ashby

150 Playing House
by Meg Hudson

156 Red, Red Roses
by Toni Anders

162 The Strength Of Love
by Em Barnard

168 Out Of The Dark
by Kate Finnemore

p141

Poetry

17 **The Feeding Station**
by Emma Canning
35 **That Morning Cuppa**
by Susannah White
44 **On Your Marks**
by B.J. Fairweather
58 **Rain, Rain**
by Ewan Smith
99 **On The Shelf**
by Judy Jarvie
138 **My Tropical Beach**
by Emma Canning
145 **Afternoon Tea**
by Sue Moos
152 **The Visitor**
by Hazel Mary Martell
164 **The Times They Are A-changing**
by Thelma Moss

J. Campbell Kerr Paintings

2 **St Kilda, Outer Hebrides**
13 **Benmore Gardens, Dunoon**
31 **Enniskillen Castle, County Fermanagh**
47 **Sidmouth, Devon**
67 **Grantham, Lincolnshire**
85 **Loch Fyne from Hell's Glen, Argyll and Bute**
109 **Horsey Windpump, Norfolk**
141 **Benarty, Fife**
167 **Stafford, England**
174 **Barmouth, Gwynedd**

Magical Olympic Moments

25 **Tokyo, 1964**
39 **Munich, 1972**
53 **Moscow, 1980**
75 **Sarajevo, 1984**
104 **Barcelona, 1992**
115 **Sydney, 2000**
127 **Athens, 2004**
135 **Beijing, 2008**
149 **London, 2012**
161 **Rio, 2016**

For Auld Lang Syne

by Jean Cullop

WE hold hands and sing "Auld Lang Syne" along with people across the world. Like us, they are celebrating the passing year.

Christmas lights cast soft shadows across the room, for we never take down the tree until Twelfth Night. This year we have not joined the family party, and this year "Auld Lang Syne" speaks to me in a special way.

"Can we sing it again, Nana?" five-year-old Lottie, asks.

She sneezes over a plate of crisps.

"Oh, dear, you do have a bad cold, Lottie."

"Sorry about the crisps, Nana. Mummy said I couldn't go to the party with a cold. I liked it with you, though. Gramps did a brilliant dance from the olden days."

I repress a shudder and remove the crisps. Lottie is a sweetie, because my husband was never a brilliant dancer.

"It's called the Twist, Lottie, and we all did funny dances in those days."

"Can you show me how to twist, Nana?"

I am saved by my husband carrying a plate of sausage rolls – germ free and straight from the oven.

Tonight I've had time to reflect and to recall other New Year's Eves, like the one when I was sixteen and in the throes of teenage rebellion.

"Mum, why do we sing that silly song every year?" I'd asked.

My mother looked up from washing dishes long enough to throw me a tea towel.

"'Auld Lang Syne' is tradition, What's your problem, Jenny?"

"It doesn't make sense!"

"It does to me. When you've finished the dishes you can get ready for tonight."

Now I was working I believed I should make up my own mind about how I spent my time. I did not want to go to the annual family bash. I would rather stay home with the Beatles long-playing record I'd been given for Christmas. I loved music.

My dad was musical and played in a brass band. He said that was proper music, but he also liked the Beatles, which was unusual in an old person.

His brass band was playing at the town hall that night and Mum was supporting him, so they wanted me to go to the party on my own.

"You'll know everyone," Mum reasoned. "You'd be bored at a brass band concert, and at Peggy's you'll have your cousin Carol for company."

"I'm not going!"

"You are," she said firmly. "Have fun, stop being difficult and don't be so serious about everything!"

My mum was small and pretty even though she was nearly forty, but she could be tough.

She loved to party and couldn't understand why I would sooner be quiet. She wasn't into brass bands, but she wanted to please Dad. It was expected of wives.

"I am serious!" I exclaimed. "When I pass my exams I shall find a job in London and live there and have a career. Nothing ever happens in this town! Why can't I stay home? It's the 1960s and women have the vote!"

"Don't be sarcastic, and you don't have the vote at sixteen," she told me. "Aunt Peggy works hard to organise this party and Dad and I have let her down."

I shrugged. Shrugging was cool. Shrugging could win arguments if done the right way, but this time it didn't work.

I stomped to my room and threw a teenage tantrum.

Although I had no siblings, my wider family was extensive. I had aunts and uncles coming out of my ears, and I had lost count of the cousins.

Half-heartedly I changed into a red, knee-length frock and back-combed my hair into Dusty Springfield flicks, then put on as much eye make-up as I thought would pass Dad's inspection.

The family get-together was always held at Aunt Peggy's huge Victorian terraced house. Like Mum, Aunt Peggy was sociable.

Dad and Uncle George were quieter. Aunt Peggy would miss Mum tonight. She'd have to find someone else to sing with her, so I would stay well out of her way.

When Dad dropped me off, the party was already in full swing. By 11 o'clock I'd had enough. You couldn't hear what anyone was saying as Aunt Peggy had turned the music up. She was doing the Twist – sort of.

I escaped to the garden and sat on a bench with a glass of fizzy pop in one hand and a plate of sausage rolls in the other.

My feet hurt. I should have listened to Mum when she told me to wear flat shoes, but I hadn't been in a listening mood.

"Can I join you?"

I jumped, startled. The fizzy pop went one way and the sausage rolls the other.

"Oh, I'm sorry," the voice said. "I'll get you replacements, shall I?"

I stared at him. What a dreamboat!

He looked older than me and had curly black hair and brown eyes. He had a strange accent, soft and lilting like the folk songs we had sung at school.

My heart skipped, bumped and skipped again. It had never done that before; certainly not with Philip at work, who was mad about cameras.

He had asked me out, but there was a limit to how many single lens reflexes and Polaroid cameras a person could take.

So what was a dark, handsome stranger with a mysterious accent doing at our family party?

I continued to stare as he introduced himself. I couldn't imagine any of the boys I knew shaking hands.

"I'm Iain McFarlane. Charlie Roberts is a friend from college. I live in Edinburgh, but my folks have gone abroad so Charlie invited me to spend New Year with his family. Do you know Charlie?"

"He's my cousin."

I looked into his brown eyes and fell in love as you only can when you are sixteen. I wished I'd had my hair done and put on my new mini dress. I opened my mouth but no words came out.

"What's your name?" he asked.

"Jenny Roberts," I squeaked.

"Are you still at school, Jenny?"

I explained that I had started work last September at a local chemist, and talking about that helped me to pull myself together.

"I'm training to do dispensing," I said proudly. "I'm learning Latin at night school. A lot of medical stuff is written in Latin, you know. What are you studying at college?"

"I'm doing teacher training. I want to work with wee ones if I can."

He seemed to be a serious person like me. Perfect!

"Dispensing is an important career. I want to do something useful. One day I shall go to London and have a career and my own flat. I want to make my own way in the world, not just get married."

I was unaware of how pompous I sounded, but very quickly he changed the subject.

"I like your dress, Jenny. Red suits your fair hair."

I wasn't used to compliments and I didn't think anything suited my mousy locks so I giggled.

He looked confused.

"Lassie, let me see if I can find you some lemonade and something to eat after I caused you to spoil yours."

"It's fine about the food. I would like a drink, though, and if Aunt Peggy catches me she'll rope me in to dance."

He grinned and did his own version of the Twist and I tried not to laugh.

"I'm no dancer," he admitted wryly. "Now, you wait here."

He disappeared into the house.

When Aunt Peggy called me back for "Auld Lang Syne" Iain still hadn't returned, and I was soon trapped in the circle between my cousin Carol and Uncle George, who had a very red face and kept getting his feet muddled.

We began the countdown and, as Big Ben chimed on the radio, we started to sing.

Uncle George pumped my arm as we moved back and forth, until at last the front doorbell rang and Aunt Peggy rescued me.

"Jenny, why don't you see who that is?"

It was better than having my arm pulled off by Uncle George, but I gasped when I saw who was at the door.

Iain McFarlane was on the step, his dark curls framed by the street lamp. He looked splendid in a kilt and was holding a lump of coal and a block of salt.

He slipped some coins into my hand.

"Ah, it's the little chemist who's going to go far! Well, here's money for luck and happy Hogmanay," Iain said, the first foot for the coming year.

I smarted. He was not the person I had thought him to be. His unkind words hurt.

After a few days Mum found out why I was so quiet. She was very understanding. I had forgotten how gentle she could be.

"Jenny, this young man is older than you and he probably has a girlfriend. There are plenty more fish in the sea."

And she was right, because Iain's words faded away when Billy from the youth club asked me out.

Then a new girl joined the staff where I worked. Her name was Enid and she worked on cosmetics.

When I first met her she had brown hair cut in a bob like Mary Quant, the fashion designer.

Two weeks later she arrived at work with buttercup-yellow tresses, pale lipstick, false eyelashes and very short skirts.

"Your hair colour's . . . um, unusual," I told her at coffee time.

She grinned.

"It's that stuff you just spray on – it goes blonde overnight. I think I put too much on. Don't you like it?"

"It's striking."

"I could do yours, if you like," she offered.

"No, thanks," I said quickly.

Enid looked disappointed, and I think it was at that moment that she embarked on a mission to improve my image.

By the following summer I had lost weight, my mousy hair was lightened to an attractive shade of honey blonde, and I wore skirts as short as hers.

On Saturday nights we went dancing. The local salon was the place for single girls to meet boys and vice versa. We had loads of dates.

I never talked about my ambitions. Once bitten was twice shy. Some things are best kept to yourself.

Mum made Enid welcome when she came to our house, but I could tell she wasn't keen on my new friend.

"You seem to have become a carbon copy of Enid," she commented.

Deep down I knew she was right.

*   *   *   *

A loud sneeze breaks my train of thought, but I linger over my memories of Enid. My best friend now lives with her daughter an hour's drive away, and my daughter-in-law Tessa drives me over to visit.

Enid hasn't changed much. She still wears the latest lipstick, paints her nails and colours her hair.

Another sneeze.

Lottie is a dainty little girl, but a head cold is a great leveller.

"Lottie, why don't you put on your pyjamas and dressing gown, then we'll snuggle down on the sofa and watch the fireworks? We have a good view of the park from here."

"Great! Santa was clever to give me that dressing-gown, Nana."

She trots off happily and I flop on the sofa. Once you start to remember the past it does not willingly leave . . .

By the time I was nineteen, skirts were shorter, heels were lower, girls wore boots and my life had changed.

I had done well at work, passing all my exams, but somehow the urgency to move to the big city was not so strong.

Our town would do for now. I would still go to the city one day, I told myself, but I wasn't ready yet. One day.

The glitter ball flickered across the dancers as Enid and I joined in with "The Locomotion". This year I'd persuaded Mum to let me cry off Aunt Peggy's New Year bash. Enid and I were set for a great night doing the things we enjoyed.

We danced the Mashed Potato, the Frug, the Shimmy, the Twist – and my favourite, the jive – all with a succession of lads.

I didn't click with any of them, but Enid seemed to be enjoying herself with my cousin Charlie who, like me, had escaped the family bash.

The band struck up "Hey Jude", which was sad because the Beatles had now gone their separate ways.

So when a tall, dark and very handsome lad asked me to dance, I didn't hesitate.

"You don't remember me, do you, Jenny?" he asked as he took me into his arms for a slow dance.

His voice sounded oddly familiar.

I allowed my long hair to swing enticingly from side to side, knowing that it would glint in the lights from the mirror ball.

"Sorry, but no, I don't." I giggled coyly.

"We met at your family's New Year party three years ago. I'm Iain McFarlane. We sat in the garden, then they needed me for first foot. Because I'm dark haired, you see . . ."

I pulled back to get a better look at him.

"It is you!" I cried. "My, you've changed."

"So have you," he replied. "You've dyed your hair and you just flirted with me! When we last met you were a very serious girl."

I was slightly offended.

"I still am, but maybe it doesn't show, Most people like the new me."

"I like it, too, but where is all that ambition?"

"I've grown up," I retorted huffily.

"Ah, well, as you are grown up, maybe I can see you home later?"

"You don't hang about, do you?" I teased.

"Oh, no, Jenny," he said seriously. "When something feels right I go after it, and this feels right. I was offered a teaching post in this area that felt right so I accepted it. Then I met you . . ."

My heart skipped again, just as it had three years ago when I was sixteen.

"Why did you laugh at me that night?" I challenged him.

"I think you scared me a bit. You were so sure of what you wanted to do with your life. You were going to work in London, yet here you are in the same town."

"Here I am," I replied, and that, too, felt right.

Two years later we were married at our local church. I wore a short white satin dress and lace veil, and Enid was my bridesmaid in a blue mini dress. Her hair was now red, but it suited her.

My son came along a year after our wedding, followed by my daughter and two more boys, and family life took over.

I hardly ever thought about London.

Raising my family and supporting Iain when he was given the head teacher's position became my priority.

Together we also sponsored orphaned children in Africa and offered help to adults who had reading difficulties.

For the first time ever I discovered the joy in not putting my own needs first.

∗   ∗   ∗   ∗

"Nana, can you keep a secret?"

Lottie is snugly warm in her new dressing-gown and Iain has made hot chocolate.

"Oh, if it's a good one."

"Well, this is so much nicer than the big party."

"We can't all like big parties." I smile.

She sounds so like me.

"Well, they're all right, but – Nana! That was your front doorbell."

When I open the door, my heart misses a beat once again, because outside stands my lovely young Iain, wearing his kilt, his dark curly hair silhouetted against the street lamp.

The hands of time have taken me back to the night we first met when I was sixteen. It can't be Iain, yet it is.

He gives me coins and a drum of own-brand table salt.

"Here's money for luck, and happy Hogmanay, Nana."

My heart thuds back to my chest as my eldest grandson, Rod, steps into the hall, looking so like his grandfather; the same dark eyes and curly hair.

"We couldn't leave you both on your own without a first foot to cheer you. How is my poorly little sister?"

"Happy New Year, Rod," Lottie cries, then sneezes. "Old Long whatever it is."

Rod hands me an envelope.

"It's a thank-you gift from Mum for looking after Lottie tonight," he explains.

"Oh, I don't need thanks. I love having her."

My hands tremble as I open the envelope. Inside is a card, and inside the card are two tickets for a theatre weekend in London.

Tessa must have known how I once planned to move there, but I have never visited the capital. It is given with thoughtful love.

"London," I breathe. "I'm going to London at last!"

Iain squeezes my hand.

"You deserve it, love. You gave up your own dreams to marry me."

The four of us hold hands once more and sing, and then they are all here: Mum, Dad, Aunt Peggy and Uncle George.

Alive in my memory, because "Auld Lang Syne" is about those we loved who have gone, and those we love who are part of our lives today.

"For auld lang syne, my dear, for auld lang syne,

We'll tak' a cup of kindness yet for auld lang syne." ■

Benmore Gardens, Dunoon

YOU don't have to go to California to see giant redwoods; just head for the Cowal peninsula in Argyll & Bute. There, seven miles from Dunoon, the entrance to Benmore Botanic Garden is through an avenue of 49 sequoias. Planted in 1863 by the then-owner of the Benmore estate, American Piers Patrick, the trees range between 50 and 54 metres high and are still not yet fully grown.

Benmore is home to a collection of fine trees, shrubs and ferns. Its 300 species of rhododendron are arranged by botanical group and geographic origin, and provide a beautiful display.

The 120-acre site, now part of the Royal Botanic Garden Edinburgh, is open to the public between March and October. ■

Wise Words

by Moira Gee

J AMIE stared gloomily at his laptop. It was no good. He'd never find a date by next Friday.

He just wouldn't go. There was no way he was turning up at the Valentine's dinner dance without a date.

He'd been full of confidence when he'd bought the double ticket at the start of the year. But, of course, he'd assumed then that he'd still be going out with Trish by February. Why would he have thought otherwise?

On New Year's Eve, Trish had started dropping subtle hints.

"Did you know Jane and Daniel are engaged? He proposed on Christmas Eve," she said.

Then she started pausing to look into the window of every jeweller's shop in town and saying how much she liked diamonds.

Jamie wasn't stupid. He knew what she was angling for, and he'd begun to wonder if perhaps, on Valentine's Day, he should put both of them out of her misery and buy her an engagement ring.

He supposed he'd better take her along to choose it, though – it would save him taking it back when it turned out that he'd bought the wrong style.

It had come as a bit of a surprise, therefore, when Trish had broken up with him by the end of January.

He still couldn't fully understand her reasons. She had thrown words like "immature" and "childish" at him, which made no sense to Jamie at all.

Well, obviously, he understood the meanings of the words, but he didn't understand why she was attributing such words to him.

All he'd ever tried to do was keep her happy: falling in with her plans, letting her choose where they went, when they went and who they went with.

His mobile pinged at that moment, interrupting his musing. He'd been expecting Steve to text.

Yo! Wanna hang 2nite?

He typed a quick reply.

Sure. Where?

Pool at Jack's Shack. 8.30.

Jamie stretched his arms above his head and exhaled. At least he

wasn't one of those saddos who didn't have any social life at all. There was always something going on.

He hadn't played pool for a couple of weeks. It would be good to meet up with the guys.

Sunday nights were pretty boring at home. Mum usually did the ironing in front of the TV, watching everything that she claimed she hadn't had time to watch through the week, which surprised Jamie because she watched TV every night.

Dad usually sat leafing through the Sunday papers, moaning about the economy, the government, the fact that he had work the next day and making plans for the day he won the lottery.

"Jamie? Tea's on the table," his mum called up to him, and he ambled downstairs.

Throughout tea, Mum and Dad indulged in a teasing argument, but Jamie was only half listening. They always argued about the same things anyway.

It was just part of their routine, he supposed, like Dad nagging him to do the washing-up and Mum moaning at him for not tidying his bedroom.

"What do you think, Jamie?"

He jolted out of his reverie. Mum was handing him a piece of chocolate cake and looking at him expectantly.

"I was asking if you'd drop in on Gran if you're going into town tonight. She left her reading glasses here this afternoon."

"Oh – yeah, sure. Thanks."

Mum's chocolate cakes were delicious and Jamie soon polished his piece off. He offered to do the dishes before he went out, but Mum grinned and said she'd let him off just this once.

She was obviously still in a good mood after her shopping spree yesterday. What was it she'd bought? It was either a shoe rack or a toaster – or was it a new wardrobe?

He couldn't remember.

By the time he'd grabbed his jacket, Dad was slumped in his armchair channel hopping, and Mum was beginning her usual wrestling match with the ironing board.

"Bye," he called to his parents, stuffing Gran's glasses case into his jacket pocket.

* * * *

Gran's flat was near the town centre, not far from where he was to meet his pals.

He rang the doorbell and heard her singing softly as she approached the door.

Gran was cool. Sometimes it surprised him to remember that she was Dad's mum.

How could such a cheerful, positive, energetic woman be the mother of such a –

"Jamie! What a lovely surprise! Come in, dear."

Jamie didn't mind putting up with Gran's hugs.

"Hi, Gran. I'm on my way out, but I've brought your glasses." He followed her into her compact kitchen.

"Thanks. Are you meeting Trish?"

"No, we – we've split up."

"Oh, dear, I'm sorry."

"Yeah, well." Jamie shrugged. "No big deal."

"Plenty more fish in the sea?"

"I suppose . . ." His voice trailed off and Gran looked at him keenly.

"Is there something on your mind, dear?"

"I just feel a bit, I dunno . . ."

"I understand." Gran looked seriously at him and his heart lifted momentarily.

"Do you?"

"No, of course I don't. You're not using proper sentences."

Jamie often forgot that Gran had been an English teacher before she retired.

"What exactly are you trying to say?" Gran put her hand on his shoulder and guided him to sit at her spotless little kitchen table.

"Well, I'm feeling a bit, you know . . ."

"No, I don't, James," she said sternly. "Use words. You're feeling a bit what?"

Jamie thought hard.

"Restless. I suppose that's the word I'm looking for."

16

The Feeding Station

FROM my window, I gaze at the garden –
Flower borders and branches are bare.
It's a bleak, barren scene and it's cold out,
With winter's harsh chill in the air.

I'm expecting some visitors shortly –
Now, who'll be the first of the day?
Then a flutter of wings in the stillness:
A goldfinch alights on the tray.

Two collared doves settle beside him:
A great tit then flits into view.
More follow, descending so swiftly:
A blackbird, a sparrow or two.

A robin hops on to the ground-dish;
One blue tit, then two, and now three!
They cling, upside down, to my feeder,
All pecking industriously.

I watch them enjoying their banquet,
See – suet balls, worms, nuts and bread.
That once-barren scene is so busy;
Yes, it's cold – but my guests are well fed!

Emma Canning

"Why? Because of Trish?"

"Not exactly. But she might have started it off by some of the things she said."

When Gran stepped away, he thought she was heading to switch on the kettle, but to his surprise, she opened the fridge and took out two small bottles of beer.

"I take it you're not driving?" she asked.

"No. Bus."

She promptly opened the bottles and handed one to him.

He grinned.

"It's the supermarket's own brand, but it's fine." Gran took a genteel sip. "Now, tell me what's on your mind."

So Jamie told her about Trish accusing him of being immature and childish.

"Why do you think she said that?" she asked once he'd finished.

"I dunno. I mean, I don't think I am those things. I'm sensible really. I'm working. I don't smoke. I'm saving up for a place of my own. I don't drink and drive or anything."

"Yes, that does all sound sensible." Gran nodded approvingly.

"Maybe it's because I still want to go out and do things with my mates." He shrugged.

"That doesn't sound unreasonable. You still saw her quite often, didn't you?"

"About three times a week." Jamie took a swig of beer. "In fact – yes, it was three times a week."

He tapped his fingers on the bottle in his hands.

"Wednesdays, Fridays and Saturdays."

"Always the same days?" Gran's eyebrows rose slightly.

"Yes. Without fail." A note of surprise crept into Jamie's voice.

"Whose idea was that?"

"I think it just happened," he replied doubtfully. "At least – well, it certainly wasn't my idea. It does sound boring, though, doesn't it?"

"Some people like routine," Gran replied diplomatically.

A mental picture of his parents flashed into Jamie's mind. Sure, they seemed happy enough in their own world, squabbling about conservatories and television quizzes, but . . .

He suppressed a shudder.

"You seemed to be getting along well," Gran remarked.

"I thought we were," he agreed, "but she obviously changed her mind."

"Why was that, do you think?"

"A couple of her friends got engaged recently." He shrugged. "One on her twenty-first – another at Christmas."

"But you weren't thinking the same?"

"No!" Jamie felt a familiar panic rising within his chest. "No, I wasn't! I think that's what miffed her."

He slumped gloomily over the table.

"But if she'd waited till next week! I mean, it's Valentine's Day and I thought I'd better . . ."

"You thought you'd better what?"

"Well, it seemed the only way to keep her happy."

"James!"

Jamie stopped abruptly. Gran was looking almost as fierce as Trish had looked on the night she'd dumped him.

In fact, now that he thought about it, Trish had always looked fierce.

He tried to concentrate on Gran again. She seemed to be trying very hard not to shout at him.

Trish had never bothered to try. She'd just shouted at him whenever she felt like it, which was quite often.

"You were going to get engaged because 'you thought you'd better'? Because it seemed the only way to keep her happy?"

"Well, yeah."

"Not because you wanted to?"

"Well, no, but I thought she wanted –"

"Not because you couldn't imagine life without her?"

"No, of course I . . ." Jamie stopped in the middle of his half-thought-out answer.

"Call me old-fashioned, but I always thought that was the reason for becoming engaged."

Gran was smiling softly and for a second she looked unexpectedly like his dad. He'd never noticed it before.

"So, how is life without Trish?" she asked, interrupting his thoughts. "Just think about it for a minute."

Jamie did as he was told. He remembered sitting outside changing-rooms in town while Trish tried on 14 outfits, all of which she then claimed made her look fat.

He remembered how irritated she'd become if he watched football on TV; how petulant she'd be with him if he was late in phoning her, or if he suggested seeing a different kind of film at the cinema.

Now he could watch what he liked and go out with his mates, who didn't give him a hard time for not phoning. He could avoid shopping for the rest of his life if he felt like it.

After a minute, he came to the conclusion that life without Trish wasn't too bad. Life without Trish was quite good, actually.

To be truthful, life without Trish was a lot better than life with Trish!

"Well?"

Jamie drew in a shaky breath.

"Wow! Gran, I think I've had a lucky escape." He grinned at her in relief. "I'm not ready for that sort of commitment, am I? What was I thinking?"

"There's no rush," Gran agreed. "Perhaps you need more time to grow up. Perhaps that's what Trish meant when she said the things she said."

Jamie stood up, looking a lot happier.

"I'll have to get going, Gran. I'm playing pool with some mates." He gave a short laugh. "Trish always hated that. Looks like she's done me a favour after all."

"It's possibly best for you both, if you're not on the same wavelength," Gran said tactfully. "You have plenty of time."

"OK, well, thanks for the beer, Gran."

"You're welcome. Oh, Jamie – my glasses?"

Jamie dug his hand into his pocket and brought out the case. Something else fluttered to the floor.

Jamie glanced down.

"Just chuck that, Gran. I won't be needing it any more." He laughed. "See you later."

The door closed behind him and Gran looked at the ticket in her hand.

A double ticket for the Valentine's dance in the town hall.

An evening of music and romance for all ages.

A smile spread slowly across her face.

"Well, if you won't be needing it, my boy . . ."

She took another sip of beer and picked up her phone. ■

A Precious Gift

by Jan Snook

TOMORROW was Mother's Day. Another year that she wouldn't have a card.

When Amelia started school, Katie thought, things would be better. School would deal with things like making Mother's Day cards, wouldn't it?

At the moment Amelia was only three, and she didn't go to nursery every day, so they'd probably made cards on one of the days Amelia was at home.

If Henry were still around, he would have bought a card and helped Amelia to write her wobbly name in it. He would have taken Amelia out to buy some flowers, or maybe picked some from the garden.

But Henry had died in a sailing accident just before Amelia was born.

Katie clenched her fists, still angry at the futility of it all. You'd have thought that Father's Day would be the difficult day, and Henry's birthday, Christmas and Amelia's own birthday. Any of them.

But it was Mother's Day that hurt.

Did that make her a selfish person, Katie wondered. It was a day when she really needed company to stop her feeling so sorry for herself.

Her own mother lived too far away, and Mother's Day wasn't a day she could easily invite people round. Everyone would be busy.

An invitation would remind them that she wasn't busy and then they'd feel sorry for her. Which was definitely not what she needed.

Katie went upstairs on impulse and tiptoed into Amelia's room, where a night light illuminated the roundness of her daughter's cheeks, her mouth slightly open, one hand clutching a pink rabbit.

She looked so carefree, Katie thought as she drew the covers up and kissed her daughter lightly on the cheek.

The phone began to ring, but Amelia didn't stir.

"Hello?" Katie answered, slightly out of breath and grateful for the interruption to her wave of self-pity.

"Katie, I know it's not much notice," her friend Annabelle began, "but are you and Amelia free to come over to lunch tomorrow? My parents

Illustration by Gerard Fay.

will be here, and Luke would love someone to play with."

"But it's a family party," Katie began.

"There will just be the eight of us," Annabelle said quickly, "and we'd love to have you."

She paused.

"You know Robert finds my father a bit overwhelming. You'd be doing us a real favour."

Katie and Annabelle had met on their first day at art school, and had been best friends ever since. Much too long for Katie to believe the "doing us a favour" bit.

"Oh, Annabelle, you're a lifeline," Katie admitted gratefully. "Can I bring a pudding or anything?"

"No," Annabelle said firmly. "Just yourselves. See you tomorrow."

It wasn't until she was off the phone that Katie went over what Annabelle had said.

Annabelle, her husband Robert and three-year-old Luke would be there, obviously, and Katie's parents made five. She and Amelia would make it seven. So who was the eighth guest?

Annabelle was good at picking up waifs and strays – she and Amelia were a case in point, Katie reflected ruefully. Perhaps there was someone else who needed mothering on Mothering Sunday?

The following day Katie and Amelia picked a posy of flowers from the garden, then walked the short distance to Annabelle's house, where Katie picked up Amelia so that she could reach the bell.

They were ushered in, the posy was handed over, the children disappeared upstairs to play and Katie felt the warmth of their welcome wash over her.

It was lovely to be out. A wonderful smell of roast lamb was coming from the kitchen, and Katie followed Annabelle there.

"What can I do to help?" she asked.

"Do you think you could stir the gravy?" Annabelle asked, handing Katie a wooden spoon. "There's something I must do upstairs. I'll only be a moment."

Katie stirred the gravy obediently, only looking up when the doorbell rang again.

"It's me," a deep voice said, already having let himself in. "Annabelle, how are –?"

He stopped dead in the kitchen doorway.

"Well, either my sister's changed out of all recognition, or it's Katie, isn't it?" he said, a grin replacing his initial look of surprise.

"I'm Annabelle's brother, Simon," he added, sticking out a hand. "I don't suppose you remember, but we met when you and Annabelle were at art school."

"Oh, there you are, Simon," Annabelle said, coming back in at that moment. "You remember Katie, then?"

Her eyes were sparkling and Katie's heart sank.

Was she being set up? This seemed to be happening a lot recently, together with gentle enquiries about whether she might be ready to start socialising again.

Socialising? They meant dating, of course. And it was all very kindly meant, she knew that, but she wasn't sure that she'd ever feel ready.

She hardly glanced at Simon, concentrating on the gravy to cover her confusion, and was taken aback when she looked at him properly to see how good-looking he was.

He wasn't just good-looking – he was gorgeous.

It struck her that she hadn't taken in anyone's looks for years.

She became conscious of Annabelle's amused expression, and found herself blushing.

"Simon's an artist," his sister said, "and, unlike the rest of us, he actually manages to make a proper living out of it."

Simon gave a self-deprecating laugh.

"I'm in a well-paid industry," he said apologetically. "My day job's in advertising."

"He's being too modest," Annabelle said. "He's been abroad for years, but he's just got a job over here as the art director for a big agency. Your portraits are selling really well, too, aren't they, Simon? He's got loads of commissions."

"Portrait painting is what I really love," he explained to Katie, "but mortgage companies feel happier if you've got a regular income – hence the advertising job. Anyway, I'd better go and say hello to my favourite nephew," he said, before disappearing upstairs.

"Have you seen that new beer ad?" Annabelle asked, peering into the oven before mentioning a well-known brand. "Simon did all the artwork for that. He's brilliant, he really is."

She turned back towards Katie with a mischievous smile.

"So what do you think of him?" she whispered.

"He's your brother, so I'm sure he's great." Katie smiled, turning back to the gravy. "Shall I turn this off, or are we about to eat?"

"You go and have a drink. We'll be ready soon."

Katie went into the sitting-room to talk to Annabelle's parents, and not long afterwards Annabelle called them to the table.

"Luke, Amelia!" she called up the stairs. "Time for lunch."

The meal was a very jolly affair, with everyone talking at once and a great deal of laughter.

By the time they'd finished pudding, Katie was feeling totally relaxed and happy. Annabelle and Robert were good hosts, her parents were interested in everything, and Simon was very good company.

"I think these little ones could do with a walk as soon as we've cleared up," Robert said as the volume from Luke and Amelia's end of the table grew louder. They were clearly very excited about something.

"Yes," Annabelle's mother said. "Why don't all you young ones go for a walk, and Dad and I will clear up? When you get back we can have a cup of tea."

Despite everyone's objections, before long Annabelle's mother was wearing an apron, her father was clearing the table and the rest of them were putting on jackets.

The children were running back and forth, stopping to examine stones and beetles and leaving the adults free to talk amongst themselves as they walked.

Annabelle engaged her husband in an intense conversation about whether or not they should go to Cornwall in the summer, causing Simon to look at Katie knowingly.

"I have the distinct feeling that my sister intends us to get to know each other," he said.

Katie opened her mouth to reply, but he smiled and continued.

"Which fortunately is just what I want to do."

He told her all about the cottage he'd just bought, his job, a film he'd been to see the night before, and he made her laugh with stories about the people he'd painted recently.

"Annabelle tells me you work from home," he said enquiringly. "How's that going?"

"I freelance," Katie replied. "Mostly I do designs for greetings card companies," she added slightly defiantly. "It's not fine art, but I needed a job I could combine with looking after Amelia, and I don't do that badly out of it. I'm well aware I'm not in your league."

Her voice changed from defiant to wistful.

"You did that portrait of Luke that's in Annabelle's sitting-room, didn't you? It's sublime."

To her surprise he stopped walking and faced her.

"I'm glad you like it. But why are you sounding so apologetic for your own work? I don't know how mothers manage to get anything done, with juggling work and childcare. Particularly when they're . . . Anyway," he added quickly, seeing her expression, "Annabelle says you draw beautifully, and she's not easily impressed."

They had walked a circular route and were nearly back at Robert and Annabelle's house when Amelia, looking troubled, ran back to Katie and Simon.

Katie put her arms out, but it was Simon whose ear Amelia whispered in.

"Don't worry, Amelia, there's still plenty of time," he said as she took his hand.

The lump in her throat was back, Katie realised, but they would soon be drinking tea and eating cake, and quite soon the whole Mother's Day thing would be over.

To her surprise, this thought was not as comforting as she expected.

"Up you go, Amelia," Annabelle was saying, ushering Amelia and Luke upstairs as soon as they arrived home. "Don't forget this time."

"But I don't know which one to bring," Amelia said, looking puzzled.

At this, Annabelle looked perplexed, but Amelia was already halfway up the stairs.

When she came back down, together with a broadly grinning Luke, she was clutching three cards in her chubby hands.

"Happy Mother's Day!" she and Luke shouted in unison.

"What's this, Amelia?" Katie asked, hoping her voice sounded normal.

"Look!" Amelia said happily, thrusting a card with a felt-tip drawing of a bunch of flowers on the front into Katie's hands. "This is the one me and Luke maked! I drew it all by myself!"

"And she's how old?" Simon asked seriously, examining the card. "You've obviously got another artist in the family."

"And this one I writed my name in!" Amelia continued excitedly. "Annabelle helped me."

"I didn't realise she and Luke were making one," Annabelle said apologetically, "or I wouldn't have interfered."

"And neither would I," Simon said apologetically, as Katie stared at the third card.

"But you were only gone for five minutes," Katie said, remembering Simon had gone up to say hello to Luke before lunch. "I shall really treasure . . ."

She stopped, still looking at the last card. It was a pencil sketch of Amelia – no more than a few lines, really.

"You've totally caught her. It's incredible. I can't wait to have it framed."

"I'd like to do a proper portrait, if you'd let me," Simon said quietly, as the others oohed and aahed over the picture of Amelia.

"I'd love a proper portrait of Amelia," Katie said sincerely, "but I doubt I could afford you. No wonder you're doing so well. It's brilliant."

"I certainly didn't mean a commission," Simon said, touching her hand. "I would really like another chance to paint Amelia, but what I meant was that I'd like to paint you. While I get to know you better." ■

Magical Olympic Moments

1964

When Ann Packer, a PE teacher from Reading, arrived at the Summer Olympics in Tokyo, the twenty-two-year-old was a firm favourite to win the 400m. The optimism was warranted, due to the fact Packer had already run the fastest time in the world over that distance earlier in the year.

Although the young runner didn't disappoint, earning a silver in the event, she really made her mark in sporting history by scooping gold in the 800m race. The win was unexpected – Packer had never previously run an international 800m race before. Not only that, she astounded everyone by doing it in 2:01.1, a world-record time.

Packer dedicated her debut Games success to her fiancé Robbie Brightwell, who was also competing in the Games – and she completed her race by running straight into his arms. The pair were married shortly afterwards. Other medallists to bring back gold for Britain were Ken Matthews in the men's 20km walk, Lynn Davies in the men's long jump and Mary Rand in the women's long jump. ∎

A Life In Rhyme

by Natalie Kleinman

MARGO BRAITHWAITE started writing poetry when she was six years old. She began with rhyming couplets.

I wunce saw a little grey bunny
When he jumpt I thawt it was funny

Not Wordsworth, perhaps, and the spelling was questionable, but the scansion was always perfect.

She tried illustrating her poems as well. Her success at drawing rabbits and dogs fell far short of her ability to put words together.

One day in school, during reading practice, her teacher asked each child to read aloud to the rest of the class.

"Margo, I'd like you to recite this limerick, please," Miss Lombard said.

It was the first Margo had ever seen.

"Yes, miss," she replied a little nervously.

It was poetry; how hard could it be?

From that day on, in her eyes, she had discovered a form of poetry that could encompass a whole different world in just five lines. Margo had found her vocation.

Not very much changed over the years. She was an enthusiastic participant in every variety of sport that her school had to offer, even writing rhymes about them.

While playing the game of netball
She gave it her absolute all.
Put the ball in the net,
Then a sad fate she met
When like Humpty she had a great fall.

For a long time Margo wrote only for her own amusement and that of her parents who, like all good parents, were only too ready to listen to the products of their child's imagination.

Then she entered a school competition. She didn't win, but her poem was placed second and appeared in that year's school magazine.

One year she broke her leg – the consequence of an accident on the hockey field – and while incapacitated she wrote several sport-related limericks.

She put them together in a pamphlet. They were handwritten, photocopied, and each carried a small illustration penned by Margo herself.

She would never be an artist, but she was by then adept enough to create something that complemented her poetry. And it was the words that were of paramount importance to her.

Each Easter the village held a fair, and her mother ran the cake stall. This particular year, a small table was added to the end on which copies of Margo's pamphlet were displayed. Every single one of them sold, adding funds to the appeal – the church roof needed repairs – and pride to their creator and her family.

Margo entered the sixth form and became an A-grade student. Her hope was to go to university to study English and the history of poetry.

Living in a village, she had been brought up to think and breathe community. She would visit the local hospital and read to the patients.

Her favourite was the children's ward, but she was comfortable with the elderly – though they preferred to listen to the old favourites they had learned during their own time at school many years ago.

For a very fleeting time Margo considered nursing, but she was ill-equipped to follow such a career. No, it had to be something associated with writing or, at the very least, reading.

Margo loved university. Here she could read and write as much as she pleased. And now that she'd been able to leave behind the dreaded maths and sciences, she was happy to study.

She had her first serious romance. Arthur wanted to see the world, and invited her to join him.

"Just think of the fun we could have. Six weeks travelling. We could pick fruit. Sleep under the stars."

She quite liked the idea of spending that much time with Arthur, but sleeping under the stars was something to be done in poems, not for real. In any case, she didn't think her parents would approve.

She went home for the summer and wrote of imagined places.

The stars they do twinkle at night,
Throwing oh, so romantic a light.
In the shield of your arm
I will come to no harm
And all things will be right and tight.

Margo had to admit to herself that, while sure she hadn't made a mistake, she might perhaps have missed a golden opportunity.

Opportunity wasn't the only thing she missed. When the new term started, Arthur told her he'd met a beautiful French girl and they'd become pen pals. Swallowing her disappointment, she wished him well and moved on.

The war had been over for nearly 20 years now, and Europe had opened up. Come the next summer holiday, Margo and her friend Daisy did what so many students had begun to do in those days: travel across the English Channel to foreign climes.

They made their way to Paris, feeling very grown up, and, such is youth, displaying no little bravado.

Her parents had given her some spending money, but Margo astonished herself by standing on the bank of the Seine and reciting her poetry.

With flowing hair and equally flowing dress, a long multi-coloured scarf and fingerless gloves, she was the epitome of a child of her generation. Naturally she'd bought a beret, too, and placed it on the ground in front of her. She was in France, after all.

Daisy had been wandering up and down looking at the sights, and the only one more surprised than she was Margo herself when they found several coins had been dropped into the hat.

"Good grief, you can actually earn money from those things!"

Margo chose not to be offended, and the next few days were spent with Daisy quite happily sitting with her back to the wall watching the world go by, while Margo staked claim to a small pitch and told the world, or whoever would listen, about the beauty of the English countryside; the joy of a babbling brook; the pain of a broken heart.

On the third day, a young man stopped to listen to the latter, a rapt expression on his face.

"You have suffered like this?" he asked.

"Not exactly, but enough to understand how it must be."

"Then you have not yet met the right man."

His name was René. She introduced him to Daisy, who had been observing all from her vantage point against the wall.

"Me, I have a friend. He will come, too. You will meet us, yes?" René asked.

They agreed, and both enjoyed a holiday romance.

Three weeks into the next term, Margo met Benjamin. Benjamin was not a poet, but he was an athlete – and she had never lost her love of sport.

She watched him play; he listened to her read. They began as friends with shared interests, but friendship grew to love, and this time it was real and lasting.

They began making plans.

When Benjamin applied for and won a job writing for the sports section of a provincial newspaper, they decided to marry straight away. Their new town was no great distance from Margo's home village, and they began married life in a small rented flat close to where her parents lived.

In her final year at university, Margo started submitting her poems to a national greetings card manufacturer, and what began as a way of earning pin money became a career.

Not only that, but it was one she was able to continue after she had her first child, then her second, and then her third.

Margo missed Benjamin when his job took him away from home to cover a football game or a cricket match, but as the children grew older the whole family were able to accompany him.

They bought a second-hand car, into which a picnic was packed along with the children. They were a lively bunch, and keeping them entertained on long journeys required considerable imagination.

Peter and James loved the quizzes their parents set, usually peppered with several questions on sport. Joanna, the youngest, preferred to be tested on history and nature.

Margo and Benjamin hardly noticed the years passing by until – in no time, it seemed – the boys had left home, and Benjamin was leading his daughter down the aisle as father of the bride.

Joanne and her husband remained in the village, with Jo taking over the cake stall that her grandmother had run for so many years.

Where Margo's pamphlet had once been displayed, there were now beautiful cards of every sort carrying her poems.

The hardest thing Margo had to deal with was Peter's move to Australia, and James's move to the US.

They were able, on alternate years, to take a holiday to each of those countries, and in time met new daughters-in-law and grandchildren, but the family were never again together in one place at the same time. It was a constant regret, but one she kept to herself. What was the use of saying?

Never happy with technology, she nonetheless managed to master the basics of using a computer, particularly for its ability to connect her in real time with her far-flung relations.

She was able to watch the children grow up, and to talk to them – something that was a precious gift when she and Benjamin were no longer able to undertake the long journeys to the other side of the world.

Life had been good to Margo, and she continued to write into her old age. It was a compulsion she in no way wanted to resist, and while she'd never been very good at baking cakes, she took pride in her ability to create something of a different sort.

Joanne's daughter, Emily, was eighteen and preparing to go to university, just as Margo had so many years ago. Though she hadn't yet taken her end-of-year exams, it seemed there was little doubt she would gain a place.

Easter had come around again, with Joanne manning the cake stall, and Margo holding court at her small table.

It was harder to sell cards these days. So many people sent their greetings online, but there were still those who liked the more personal touch.

Emily came to sit beside her.

"I can't believe I'll be going away soon, Gran. I'm going travelling with friends during the summer, so I won't see much of you – though I'll be back for a week before term starts."

Margo thought back to the time she had taken her first trip and met – what was that boy's name? René? How long ago that was!

"I've got something for you, Gran. I want you to think about me when I'm gone, and know I'll be missing you."

Margo was touched, though she knew Emily would probably be too busy with her own life to think much about her old gran.

"Here, take it," Emily said, handing her an envelope. "I made it myself using a program on my computer."

There was a card with a simple drawing on the front – not dissimilar to Margo's own attempts at illustration – but it was the words inside that touched her heart.

I want you to know 'cause it's true
And it's something the world should know, too:
You're the best gran to me
You could possibly be –
You're my rock and I truly love you.

Margo looked up at her granddaughter with tears unashamedly falling down her cheeks, but she was smiling.

Emily wiped a tear away with her finger.

"Happy Easter, Gran." ■

Enniskillen Castle, County Fermanagh

THE castle, on the banks of the River Erne in Northern Ireland, was built in 1428. It withstood conflict and sieges down the centuries, being strengthened in 1796 to respond to the threat of a French invasion. It was a barracks for a succession of regiments, most recently the North Irish Horse, a Territorial Army unit.

In 1950 it was decommissioned, and today it houses two museums and a heritage centre. The Inniskillings Museum is the regimental museum of the Royal Inniskilling Fusiliers and the 5th Royal Inniskilling Dragoon Guards.

The Fermanagh County Museum exhibits the area's history, traditional rural life and local crafts, with a section devoted to Belleek Pottery, one of the county's main products since 1863. ■

Hidden Treasure

by Samantha Tonge

D EBORAH yawned as little Edie pulled her excitedly towards
the park.

Why did the Brownies' charity Easter treasure hunt have to
start at nine o'clock on a Sunday morning – the one day of the
week she was guaranteed a lie in?

"Nine o'clock isn't that early, Mum," nine-year-old Edie said, as if able
to read her thoughts. "It's a perfectly reasonable time for people who
don't stay up all Saturday night watching box sets."

She shook her finger.

Deborah couldn't help grinning. Sometimes her daughter behaved like
the mother.

Edie had been sensibly tucked up by half-past eight the previous
evening, full of excitement about the following morning's promise of
running around the park and eating chocolate.

Deborah, on the other hand, had gone back into the lounge and had
settled down in front of the television to enjoy a box set of vampire
romance.

Since being promoted to store manager, she rarely got Saturdays off
and was immensely grateful to her parents for babysitting at the
weekend.

She had become used to spending evenings on her own. Dating
proved hard with a full-time job and a young daughter.

For the moment, Deborah had given up on finding "the one".

She had tried speed-dating and had gone on blind dates, but enough
was enough. It was less disheartening to stop looking.

In any case, Edie was her priority.

Her grin widened because "perfectly reasonable" was the latest adult
phrase Edie had picked up.

Last night she'd used it to describe her fish fingers and chips.

Illustration by Martin Baines.

Deborah ruffled her daughter's hair. How quickly the little girl was growing up.

Whilst this early Sunday start was challenging, Deborah knew that the day would come when she would miss these mother and daughter jaunts.

She turned up the collar of her jacket as they reached the crowd of people already by the starting point, cast in the shadow of a huge willow tree.

Deborah thought back to that painful day when she was eighteen, sitting in the garden beside a very similar tree with her parents.

She had just come back from a gap year exploring the United States with her half-American boyfriend. She knew she was about to shatter the dreams they'd held for their only daughter.

Neither of them had been to university, and her parents had always talked proudly of bright Deborah obtaining a degree and seeing the world.

It had also shattered a young Deborah's hopes for a fancy life after university, with new cars, smart clothes and exotic travels.

"What's the matter?" her mum had asked. "Are you still worried about starting your studies after a year away from the academic lifestyle? You can only do your best, love. We know you'll come up trumps."

Deborah's mouth had been as dry as if she'd eaten a whole packet of crackers.

"Deborah, what's wrong? You can tell us, sweetheart," her father had said.

She'd hung her head, unable to face the disappointment she expected when she told them they would soon be grandparents. That her boyfriend – now her ex – had stayed on in America instead of returning to Britain.

* * * *

Deborah shook herself and took a map from one of the organisers, paying her five pounds to take part. The money was going to a local homeless shelter.

She handed the sheet of paper to Edie, who jumped up and down and pulled her mother's hand once more.

"Come on, Mum. I want to win the treasure chest."

They read the first clue.

We're standing together, lots of us, like members of a choir.
Our trumpets are yellow, but if I said they could play music I'd be a liar.

Deborah caught the eye of little Megan's dad.

She'd not met him before. His wife normally attended these kinds of events.

"Not obvious, is it?" He smiled with a twinkle in his eyes.

But it wasn't just any smile – for some reason it made the crisp breeze seem less cold. It forced Deborah's mouth to quirk up in return.

It made her feel less jaded and worn.

His wife was a lucky woman.

"Mum would be able to work out the answer. It's a shame she's got such a bad cold." Megan glared at her father.

Deborah caught his eye and shot him a sympathetic grin.

"We could work together," Edie suggested to Megan.

"And split the treasure!" Megan nodded vigorously and pulled down her woolly hat.

Her dad gave one of those smiles again and held out his hand.

"I'm Aidan."

"Deborah." She liked a firm handshake. "So I think we are looking for –"

"Flowers!" Edie interrupted. "Granny is always talking about those pretty ones in her garden having trumpets."

"So what sort of yellow flowers are they?" Aidan asked the girls.

"Buttercups!" Megan cried.

"Dandelions!" Edie added.

Then Megan clapped her hands.

"I know! Daffodils! We saw loads of them on the way here, by that big oak."

"Come on," Edie said, taking Megan's hand. "We have to get there before anyone else!"

That Morning Cuppa

AN early morning cup of tea,
When no-one else is up,
Always brings delight to me
Sipped from my favourite cup.

I snuggle in a cosy chair
Beside the fire's glow;
It's cold outside, but I don't care,
There's nowhere I need go.

I like my tea quite strong and hot
To welcome the new day,
And always make it in a pot –
It tastes better that way!

Susannah White

Deborah and Aidan let the girls charge off, as the two friends were familiar with the layout of the park.

They weren't quite the first to reach the carpet of yellow daffodils, but the four of them quickly solved the next clue and moved on.

Some riddles were easier for the children to work out; others needed the input of adults.

As they headed to the fourth clue, by the play park, Aidan gave a big yawn.

"Late night?" Deborah asked.

He nodded.

"I'm an assistant manager in a care home. One of our residents had food poisoning. My shift was due to finish at eleven, but I was worried and stayed a bit later to make sure the worst was over."

"Do you enjoy your job?"

His face lit up.

"It's so rewarding to see new residents settle in. Within weeks they feel more like friends. I do my best to make it a happy place."

He stepped over a fallen log.

"When I was seven, I went to boarding school. Mum and Dad thought it was for the best, as he got a promotion that meant going abroad for

iStock.

35

weeks on end with work.

"But I hated it," he continued. "I've never forgotten what it feels like to live in a place that doesn't feel like home."

"How many years were you there?"

"Only one. My parents could see how unhappy I was. Dad changed his job."

Aidan shrugged.

"So you can understand why it's very rewarding for me to see how content the residents are."

"I work with the other end of the age spectrum, spending my days selling prams and car seats. I manage a branch of Baby Bonanza," Deborah said.

She then slipped on a patch of mud and Aidan offered an arm to steady her. She took it gratefully.

They chatted about work, television shows and the weather, whilst the girls concentrated on the treasure hunt.

They were determined to solve as many of the clues as possible on their own.

Deborah discovered Aidan also liked vampire dramas and curries.

"There's nothing like a chicken tikka masala and garlic naan bread after a visit to the gym," he announced.

Deborah laughed.

"Agreed! It's my favourite — but only if you can convince yourself all those calories aren't undoing the hard work."

They reached the final clue.

"Right, let's concentrate," Deborah said, looking around. "We're in the lead, but only just."

Well done: you are almost there!

You've had clues about flowers and plants and pets.

This one concerns something that flies so prettily through the air.

Where can you find it? You might need your nets.

"Nets. You use nets to catch butterflies, and butterflies are pretty and they fly," Megan said, then began running. "I know just where to go!"

"Me, too!" Edie cried, and tore off.

"They must be heading towards the insect garden," Deborah said as she and Aidan hurried after the two of them.

The girls soon disappeared amongst the trees ahead. Chest heaving, Deborah finally arrived, and Aidan soon after.

Megan stood on her own.

"Where's Edie?" Deborah asked.

Megan looked around.

"I thought she'd got tired and waited for you. Edie?"

Deborah's heart raced as she told herself not to panic. Motherhood always made her think the worst.

No-one warned you that being a parent was scary — that you became the strictest health and safety officer when it came to your offspring.

Deborah never stopped worrying about whether Edie was content at school, eating properly or getting enough sleep.

She took a deep breath. Edie was a sensible girl.

"I'll see you later," she said to Aidan, her voice wavering. "She's probably been distracted by a squirrel, or sometimes you see rabbits here. Hopefully I'll be back with her in a minute."

"Wait!" Aidan put up his hand. "We're in this together."

He glanced at his daughter.

"Friends are more important than treasure. We'll come, too."

Megan paused for a brief moment, then nodded, her face now looking worried.

"Thanks so much," Deborah said, a nauseous sensation backing up her throat. "I wonder if she's gone back to the pond where the fishing nets are that you can hire out."

"It's definitely worth a look," Aidan replied. "It won't take us long to get there, and we can all keep our eyes peeled on the way."

The three of them hurried back to the pond, each of them scouring the scenery on their way.

They passed other parents, who said they'd keep a look-out.

"Edie? It's Mum! Where are you?" Deborah broke into a run.

"Edie, we're going to lose the treasure hunt!" Megan called.

Eventually they reached the pond. Deborah spied the nets leaning up against the park keeper's shed.

With red, blotchy eyes, Edie was sitting on the ground underneath them.

They all hurried over.

"Mummy!" Tears trickled down her cheeks. "I tripped over a big stone. My ankle hurts. I can't stand up."

Deborah crouched down and scooped her daughter into her arms.

"Shush. You're OK now." Her shoulders relaxed, but still her voice shook.

"Sorry, Megan," Edie said and gulped. "I got it wrong. We won't win the treasure now."

Megan delved into her pocket and pulled out a lollipop.

"It doesn't matter. Have this. Mummy always says a shot of sugar works wonders after a shock."

Edie smiled gratefully, and with Deborah's help stood up. The little girl winced.

"How about a piggy-back to the last clue and the treasure chest, if that's all right with your mum?" Aidan said.

"It's OK. I can do that," Deborah said, her vision still a bit blurry. "But maybe we could take it in turns? The grass makes it harder to walk with someone on your back."

"Deal," he agreed, and gave one of those smiles that immediately lifted her spirits.

"Hurry!" Megan exclaimed. "We might still win!"

They didn't win. By the time they got back, most of the Brownies had arrived.

The treasure chest had been discovered behind some large rhubarb leaves. It was full of bags of mini gold coins – enough for everyone.

After her lolly and mouthfuls of chocolate, Edie soon perked up and felt able to walk again.

"You OK?" Aidan asked Deborah as the girls led them to the swings. "That must have been frightening for you."

"Your support helped. Thank you so much."

He gave a salute and bowed.

"Any time, madam."

"Uncle Aidan, why are you being silly?" Megan shouted. "You're so embarrassing. Just like Daddy!"

Uncle? Heat swept up Deborah's neck.

He really was an attractive man – not only because of the strong arms and heart-breaking smile, but because he was funny, he was caring and, by the sounds of it, a hard worker.

It turned out Megan's dad was away on business, so Aidan had offered to step in.

His sentiment had touched her when Edie got lost.

"We're in this together."

Those were the exact same words her parents had used all those years ago when they'd found out she was expecting.

Deborah would never forget their reaction, once the initial disbelief had settled. How they'd helped her bear the responsibility of bringing a child into the world, without a partner and at such a young age, whilst at the same time encouraging Deborah not to rely on them too much.

Oh, they'd babysit whenever needed, and helped out with costs – they loved their little granddaughter to bits – but they knew that, to be the best parent and example to Edie, Deborah had to face her responsibility head on and be independent.

It had meant that she and Edie lived on a tight budget, in a small flat, but as time passed Deborah's self-respect and confidence grew and you couldn't put a price on that.

She felt immense satisfaction in knowing that she provided for her daughter – although she was wise enough never to turn down her generous parents' offer of a lovely holiday together. Last year they'd gone to Cornwall.

"Those coins were so yummy," Edie said when Deborah tucked her into bed that night. "The treasure was really well hidden."

"Valuable things often are," she said, and smiled at having spent the day thinking Aidan was Megan's dad.

He'd asked her out for a meal when it was time to leave the park, and Edie had announced that was a perfectly reasonable idea.

Megan had rolled her eyes and said grown-ups were embarrassing.

With laughter in her eyes, Deborah suggested they meet at the local curry house.

It wasn't a fancy restaurant, and she wouldn't be driving there in a swanky car. But the last nine years had taught her that real treasures had nothing to do with money and glamour.

And during today's charity hunt, she just might have found something worth a lot more. ∎

Magical Olympic Moments

1972

Timing is everything when it comes to going for gold, and no-one knows that better than Mary Peters. Having finished fourth in 1964 and ninth in 1968, Peters headed to the Summer Olympics in Munich to compete in the women's pentathlon with that top spot firmly in mind.

At the age of thirty-three, Peters could have been forgiven for thinking this was her last chance to step up on the podium to collect an Olympic gold. It was a close-knit battle between her and Heide Rosendahl, the home favourite, in the event which involved 100m hurdles, shot put, high jump, long jump and 200m.

In the end, it all came down to the final event. Rosendahl won the race, then anxious minutes passed as scores were totted up, before Peters was declared the overall winner − by 10 points.

Other British gold medallists at the 1972 Olympics included Chris Davies and Rodney Pattisson for sailing, and two equestrian golds − Richard Meade in the three-day event individual competition and Mary Gordon-Watson, Richard Meade, Bridget Parker and Mark Phillips in the three-day event team competition. ■

A Boys' Day Out

by Jan Snook

HONESTLY, Dad," Matt began as he and his father carried their pints and a couple of packets of crisps to a table in the corner of the local pub. "I don't mind Mother's Day, of course. Mothering Sunday has a long tradition, and I accept that, but Father's Day?

"It's just a load of old rubbish dreamed up by the greetings card companies, and I refuse to play their money-grubbing little game," he finished.

Henry took a sip of beer and gazed at his son over the froth.

"And?" he prompted.

"And what?"

"Why are you telling me this? You haven't sent me a Father's Day card for . . . Well, I don't know when I last had one from you. When you were ten, probably."

"But I'm not talking about you!"

"Then I'm lost. Whoever were you thinking of sending one to, if not to me?"

Matt gazed at his father in frustration.

"I'm not talking about sending one. I'm talking about Lucas. I told him I didn't agree with Father's Day cards, but later Kirsty had a bit of a go at me."

"You and Kirsty haven't been married all that long," Henry said thoughtfully. "And Lucas is obviously very attached to you. Maybe he's been looking forward to having a stepfather to send a card to. Sort of makes it official, doesn't it?"

"But I'm adopting him. The papers should come through any day now. You can't get much more official than that."

"Has Lucas been involved in any of the paperwork for that?" Henry

asked shrewdly. "Maybe a Father's Day card seems more real when you're only seven."

Matt pulled a face.

"Have you looked at any of the cards the shops are selling? They're all so soppy."

Henry looked suddenly serious.

"Just go along with it, Matt. It's just one day. See if there's a superhero movie on and take him to see it. Pretend to enjoy it."

"I'm not even sure when Father's Day is," Matt answered morosely.

"It's this Sunday," his father told him. "I got some leaflet about it from the yacht club."

He looked at Matt over his glasses.

"I threw it out, obviously, knowing your views on the subject."

"I just think," Matt began, "that if it's supposed to be Father's Day, the father in question should have some say in the matter. Don't you?"

"I do," Henry agreed, smiling. "Though I don't know that I've ever had any say in it."

Matt pulled a face, then smiled back.

"I walked right into that one, didn't I?"

*   *   *   *   *

"How was your dad?" Kirsty asked when Matt got home an hour later. "He would be pleased to see you, I expect. Anyway, supper's nearly ready. It's salad."

Matt suppressed a groan.

"Kirsty, don't get me wrong, I think your salads are fantastic, but could we eat something else occasionally? I don't know when I last saw a potato."

"Really? You didn't have any crisps in the pub?" his wife teased, smiling. "You did agree that we could both do with losing a few pounds before July. I would like to be able to sit on a beach in a bikini without feeling like a whale."

"You are the most ridiculous woman," Matt returned, grinning. "You are never going to look like a whale. It's Friday night. Couldn't we have something less healthy just this once? I bet Lucas would like something with chips."

Kirsty's face clouded.

"Lucas has already eaten, actually," she informed him. "His friend Jamie came back from school with him and stayed for tea.

"He left about an hour ago and Lucas said he was tired, so he's gone up to bed. I expect he's reading."

"I'll go up and say goodnight," Matt said.

"I should warn you, Matt, he was in a bit of a funny mood."

* * * *

When Matt came back downstairs the promised salad was on the table, along with a basket of hot garlic bread.

Kirsty had clearly relented.

"Garlic bread and you're still not smiling? What's wrong?" she asked as they sat down.

Matt sighed.

"You're right. Lucas wasn't himself at all. I've never heard him be so offhand."

Kirsty looked down at her plate.

"Offhand with Lucas usually means miserable, Matt. I think he's quite upset."

"About this Father's Day thing?"

"It's quite a big thing to him, you know, and he thinks it's because he's not your real son." She paused. "He doesn't remember his real dad. When he died we didn't get any warning. One minute he was here, and the next . . .

"Climbing accidents aren't easy to explain to a two-year-old. He's never really had a dad before."

Matt reached across and took Kirsty's hand.

"I think I'm going to have to concede defeat about Sunday." He smiled at her. "Have you got any ideas about where we might go, by any chance?"

"Oh, Matt, I was planning to spend the day gardening. Maybe you could do something with Lucas? A boys' day out?"

"OK." Matt nodded slowly. "If Lucas is speaking to me by then."

Kirsty smiled.

"He will be. You know he adores you. Just don't expect a card. He made one at school, but then he screwed it up and threw it into the bin, I'm afraid."

∗   ∗   ∗   ∗

Sunday morning dawned bright and sunny, and it promised to be warm as well.

"I think you'd better bring a jacket or a fleece or something," Matt said as they prepared to leave. "It can be quite chilly where we're going."

"Chilly?" Lucas asked, stomping off to find a coat.

Eventually they were both in Matt's car and heading off, Matt making cheery comments and Lucas giving monosyllabic replies.

"Where are we going?" Lucas asked.

"The seaside."

"But we haven't brought our swimming things or anything!" Lucas spluttered.

"The sea's still jolly cold in the middle of June," Matt said.

"So what are we going to do?"

"Just wait and see. Though I think it might involve some fish and chips!"

"I thought Mum said you weren't allowed chips," Lucas returned, his eyes wide.

"It's a boys' day out. And a Father's Day treat," Matt declared, shrugging.

He was rewarded with a small smile – the first he had seen all weekend.

Half an hour later Matt turned into a large car park.

"What's this place?" Lucas asked, then saw a sign. "Marina and Yacht Club?"

"We're meeting Grandpa here," Matt said, helping Lucas out of the car. "It's his Father's Day, too, remember," he added, seeing the surprise on Lucas's face.

"But you don't believe in Father's Day."

Matt rolled his eyes at him.

"But you do, and your mother does, and I have a sneaky feeling that even my old dad does! I've been out-voted!"

Henry was standing by the reception desk inside the clubhouse, filling in a form.

"I've got to sign you both in as my guests," he explained. "You're wearing a jacket, so that's good. It can be a bit breezy out on the water."

"Come for the Father's Day races, have you, Henry?" the man behind the desk asked. "Great day for it."

"We're going out in a boat?" Lucas asked, and Matt saw that his eyes were shining.

Trust his dad to come up with something so perfect.

"Our race isn't until eleven o'clock," Henry stated, "so let's get some pastries and coffee and I'll tell you a bit about what's going to happen.

On Your Marks

THE gloves and the shears at the ready,
The pad that I kneel on is set.
The trowel and hoe, the spade that will go
Dig the blooms for the winning rosette.

Whilst potting the tulips and crocus,
The hyacinths perfume this place.
Now daffodils shoot their springtime salute
For the start of the gardening race.

I'm sure that I'm on to a prize win.
I've practised all winter, you see.
The starting point set, I'll never forget
That the gardening trophy's for me!

B.J. Fairweather

Three of us is going to be a bit of a squash in my boat, but I'm sure we'll manage just fine."

The next two hours went by like lightning, Matt thought with a smile, as he watched his father initiate Lucas into the etiquette of sailing, showing him the ropes (literally), teaching him what the boom and rudder were, what port and starboard meant and finding him a lifejacket.

Matt had never seen Lucas so absorbed, and Henry was clearly delighted to have such an enthusiastic pupil.

They were lucky, he thought, to have such a calm sea, with just enough breeze to make it fun.

His father's boat was small and old, intended for Henry to sail solo, but Lucas was thrilled with it.

"And the boat belongs to Grandpa?" he kept saying over and over again.

"It does at the minute," Henry said, "though I'm considering selling it. Anyway, it's time for the off so we'd better go."

It seemed the race had barely started before they were crossing the finish line, and Lucas talked excitedly the whole time while they watched the final race.

"That was so exciting!" he exclaimed, holding Henry's hand as they headed back to the clubhouse. "When can we do it again? Next time I want to win!"

"I thought we did pretty brilliantly coming third," Matt replied, laughing.

"I've just got to go and see the commodore," Henry said once they'd sat down for lunch.

"He's like the managing director of a yacht club," he added to Lucas. "I'll be back in a tick."

Lucas gazed round at the formal dining-room, where the walls were decorated with lots of pictures of various sailing boats, and where a large oak honours board listed the winners of various races over the years.

"Grandpa's name is on the honours board!" he exclaimed, and his eyes were shining with pride as he watched Henry returning to their table, smiling broadly and holding an envelope.

"Fish and chips!" Henry cried, eyeing the food which had just arrived at their table. "My favourite.

"Cheers," he added, lifting his glass. "Happy Father's Day!"

"Oh, I nearly forgot," Matt said, putting his hand in his pocket and pulling out an envelope. "Happy Father's Day."

"A card?" Henry said, surprised. "But you don't believe in –"

"Yeah, yeah," Matt said, looking shamefaced. "But Kirsty wouldn't hear of you not getting a card."

"In our house, Mum's the boss," Lucas said seriously, making them all laugh. "I made you a card, too, Dad," he added sadly, looking up at Matt, his face troubled. "But I threw it away when I was cross.

"Jamie said he and his dad were going to a film for Father's Day, and I thought we weren't doing anything." His face brightened. "Wait till I tell him about sailing!"

Matt put his hand in his pocket and pulled out another, very crumpled card, which had been flattened out as much as possible.

"Would this be it?" he asked, smiling.

"But it's ruined!" Lucas objected.

"Not at all," Matt said. "It may not be stiff and flat like the sort of cards women buy, but it's a perfect boys' card – not too neat and fussy. It's even got a picture of a boat on it. How clever is that?"

They looked up as someone tapped a glass for silence, and everyone went quiet.

"While you're all enjoying your lunch, I'd just like to announce the winners of the Father's Day races."

"We got a cup!" Lucas was still saying as the men finished their coffee half an hour later. "Just for coming third. A proper cup!"

"Thanks, Dad," Matt said, looking at the minute silver cup that Lucas was cradling. "We couldn't have had a better Father's Day. Lucas is obviously cut out to be a sailor. It's been totally brilliant."

"We must do it again soon," Henry replied, smiling.

"But how can we if you sell your boat? You won't, will you, Grandpa?" Lucas asked, his eyes pleading.

"Well, I think I may have to," Henry admitted. "Before I forget, I got a card for you, too, Lucas. So now we've got a card each." He handed the envelope that was still on the table to Lucas, whose eyes widened with glee.

"A membership card? For the yacht club?"

"It's just a temporary one, until they send you the real one," Henry explained with a grin. "I thought it would be a good idea to get family membership.

"I think," he added, "if we're going to enter the regatta in September, we should sell the boat and buy something a bit bigger. What do you think?"

"I think you're the best dad in the world." Matt smiled at his father. "And the best grandpa, too." ■

Sidmouth, Devon

A POPULAR Devon seaside town, Sidmouth lies on the famous Jurassic Coast World Heritage Site. It's hard to imagine that ancient reptiles roamed here 235 million years ago. The evidence is there in the exhibits in the Sidmouth Museum, where the fossilised footprints of the dinosaurs that first trod the beach can be seen today.

There has been a settlement in this part of the Sid valley for well over a thousand years. The town appeared in the Domesday Book as "Sedemuda" (mouth of the Sid). It became fashionable as a seaside resort during the Georgian and Victorian eras.

Sidmouth is still a favoured destination for visitors drawn by its clean, family-friendly beaches, independent shops and abundance of sporting and leisure activities. The surrounding countryside is located within the East Devon Area of Outstanding Natural Beauty, with many fine walks just on the doorstep. ∎

Old School

by Donald Lightwood

I N the summer of 1970, Julia and Avril were on their first holiday since becoming primary school teachers. They thought themselves adventurous, choosing to cycle in rural France.
Provided with bikes, they rode through beautiful countryside while their suitcases were transported ahead.

They loved the village hotels they stayed in, which were usually quaint and invariably had good food.

They arrived at Eguzon in the late afternoon, and were glad to shower and change, looking forward to dinner. Happily, they'd noticed this was to be served on the terrace at the front of the small hotel.

Following the delicious smell from the kitchen, they made their way downstairs to find the terrace crowded with diners.

Julia spotted a table with only one woman.

"Over here, quick!" she told Avril. She bent to the lady. "May we join you?"

"*Bien sûr*. Yes, of course," she replied.

They guessed she was in her early sixties.

"You are English?"

"Scottish, actually," Avril replied. "Our French isn't up to much, I'm afraid. Sorry."

The woman smiled.

"No matter. It is a good excuse for me to practise my English. My name is Beatrice Cessac."

The two introduced themselves.

"We're on a cycling holiday," Julia told her.

"You must be brave and strong," Madame Cessac said. "The last time I was on a *vélo*, I fell off."

"It's a good way to see the countryside."

"*Oui*, this is a lovely part of the world."

"How lucky you are, living here." Avril smiled.

Madame nodded.

"Yes. I came to live here with my husband, who was born in the village."

"*Bonsoir, madame!*" several passers-by called out to her.

She smiled and acknowledged them.

"Former pupils," she explained to the girls.

"You were a teacher?"

Illustration by Ruth Blair.

"Yes. At the village school."

"So are we," Julia said. "Teachers, I mean."

"I have been – how do you say? – *retraite* for some years."

"Retired," Julia suggested.

"*Oui*." Madame Cessac nodded. "The school is now a museum. I look after it."

"It must be full of memories."

"Very many." She shook her head. "Sometimes I expect the children to come in. Age plays tricks on you."

"I must say, your English is very good," Avril commented.

"It improved during the Occupation," Madame explained. "I was the only person in the village who could translate the messages on the BBC."

"Wasn't that dangerous?"

"Possibly. But, as you say, we got away with it."

"Wow!" Julia exclaimed.

The French woman frowned.

"I beg your pardon?"

"It's just a word that means I'm astonished."

"In the classroom, the children were corrected if they did not use proper French." Madame Cessac laughed.

The girls grinned.

"We do our best, but we don't always succeed," Avril admitted.

After dinner, Madame Cessac asked if they would like to look at the old school.

The girls were delighted, and arranged to meet her there in the morning.

*   *   *   *

Surrounded by a field of sunflowers, the old school building looked idyllic. Compared with the girls' school in Edinburgh, it was like something out of a fairy tale.

"It would have been heavenly working here," Julia mused.

Avril nodded.

"There must have been a downside, though."

"Maybe. But I can't imagine what it would have been."

Madame Cessac welcomed them into the classroom. The children's desks were in pairs, overlooked by an upright teacher's desk.

There were examples of the pupils' work pinned on the walls – carefully coloured pictures and pieces of writing. Everything appeared neat and correct.

On the blackboard, the Lord's Prayer was written out in a perfect script.

Even though they were teachers themselves, the two from Scotland found it hard to picture the children who had attended here.

"It must have been difficult, having pupils at different ages and stages," Julia said to Madame Cessac.

"Yes. They had to be disciplined to get on with their own work while I attended to others."

"I don't think I could manage that," Avril said doubtfully.

"At all levels they were expected to do their best. And to work hard at their behaviour, as well as their lessons."

"There must have been some misbehaviour?" Julia asked.

Madame Cessac smiled.

"Of course, and it was punished."

"How?"

She shrugged.

"A smacked hand, and sometimes for the very naughty, I used the *bonnet d'âne*."

She opened a cupboard and took out what looked like a hat with donkey's ears. It was made of papier-mâché.

"An ass's hat!" Avril cried. "*Bonnet d'âne.*"

"*Exactement.*"

"It's what we call a dunce's cap," Julia explained.

"If you were naughty, or did bad work, you had to walk round the village wearing it on your head," Madame Cessac told them.

The girls looked at each other.

"That was rather cruel, wasn't it?" Avril asked.

"It stopped them misbehaving."

"Even so," Julia put in. "Humiliating them like that . . ."

"It had always been used, since the school opened in the last century," Madame Cessac replied.

"Do they have one in the new school?" Julia asked.

The old French teacher smiled.

"I don't think so. There are new methods of keeping discipline."

"I should hope so!" Avril laughed.

"Hitting pupils used to be done in Scottish schools," Julia went on. "My dad got the tawse several times."

Madame Cessac's eyebrows raised.

"*Qu'est-ce que ça?*"

"You put your hand out and the teacher hit it with a leather belt," Julia explained.

"That would be painful," Madame said. "How do you punish children now?"

Julia and Avril shrugged and pulled a face at each other.

"They are given extra work, or sent to the head teacher," Avril replied finally.

"Being on my own, I did not have that luxury," Madame Cessac explained, running her hand over the bonnet. "It was a punishment that lived in the memory."

She smiled to herself, and pointed to a small plaque screwed on to the wall.

"This commemorates the opening of the school as a museum by the mayor." She tapped his name. "Not a popular man in the village. He behaved as if he were a minister, rather than the local mayor. Full of wind.

"He was a former pupil, and he remembered having to wear the *bonnet d'âne*. He said he had hated me, and he would have given anything to inflict the same punishment on me."

"I'm not surprised," Julia said. "You must admit it was harsh."

Madame Cessac gave another shrug.

"It was the way things were in those days."

"Thank heavens they've changed," Avril declared.

"Yes, that is true. However, for me, the bonnet brought about a change I never expected."

"What was that?"

The three looked at the battered dunce's cap, the girls wondering how the miserable object could have had any merit whatsoever.

"Strange as it may seem, I granted the mayor his wish," Madame continued. "After the opening ceremony, I told him I would walk around the village wearing the *bonnet d'âne*."

"Good heavens!" Julia exclaimed.

"How did he respond?" Avril asked.

"He was surprised, of course, and he didn't believe me. So I repeated my offer.

"Then I put the bonnet on my head, opened the door and walked out."
The girls could not restrain a giggle. The picture conjured up in their minds was bizarre.

Madame Cessac went on.

"He followed me, and people gathered as if the circus had come to town. By the time we got to the village square there was a large crowd, and they were all laughing.

"I stopped outside the church, took off the *bonnet d'âne* and handed it to the mayor. The crowd's laughter turned into cheers."

The girls regarded her with the same question on their minds.

"But why did you do it?" Julia asked.

"That's a good question." Madame laughed. "Impulse. I don't know how to describe my feelings at the time. I suppose I was angry. His pomposity always annoyed me.

"I wanted to show him that it was such a little thing that he had made so much of all these years. I doubted if what I was doing – little more than a joke – would make much difference. But it did."

The girls nodded slowly, understanding.

"I saw that he had been humiliated, as though he had been wearing the *bonnet d'âne*, not me. He had been punished by his old teacher again!

"He was strangely silent, and he left the village square without a word. People congratulated me and I walked home, feeling rather smug, I confess."

"What a remarkable story," Avril commented.

Madame Cessac nodded.

"What happened next was even more remarkable for me. You see, I came originally from Paris, and the villagers had never been sure about me. And it didn't change after I became a widow."

She shrugged lightly.

"I'm afraid that being suspicious of outsiders is typical in these small places. But after my march around the village wearing the *bonnet d'âne*, things changed. The episode won me many friends."

"We had noticed that when we were having dinner last night," Julia replied.

"It also changed the mayor, though," Madame Cessac went on. "He became far less self-important, which was much appreciated by everyone."

"And his schoolboy grudge against you?" Avril asked. "Did he forget that?"

The elderly woman's smile answered her question, but she replied nevertheless.

"Yes, he did. In fact, we have dinner together fairly often."

She patted the *bonnet d'âne* fondly, before putting it back in the cupboard.

"I keep this thing safe, just the same. And if the mayor should happen to get on his high horse about anything, well, I just remind him of our old ass's hat!" ▪

Magical Olympic Moments

1980

Due to a boycott, the Moscow Olympics attracted fewer competitors than the previous event, with around 5,000 athletes representing 81 countries. Britain managed to win four golds in athletics and one in swimming, for Duncan Goodhew.

Allan Wells won the men's 100 metres, while Daley Thompson displayed his prowess as a top decathlete, securing first place.

However, the duo that were to captivate the nation were great track rivals Sebastian Coe and Steve Ovett, and the nation eagerly awaited the showdown between the athletes, who were both at their very peak.

Deservedly, each came away with a gold: Ovett was first over the line in the 800 metres, and Coe clinched top spot in the 1500 metres.

The real surprise of this was that in the lead up to the Games, Coe held the world record in the 800 metres – so had been expected to win this event – while Ovett was better over the mile mark – the 1500 metres event being just short of this. ∎

The Whole Picture

———— by Annie Harris ————

I REREAD the letter from Jo, my longest-standing friend.
Dear Pat,
I saw these aerial town map jigsaws advertised in a magazine and
remembered how we used to enjoy doing them on wet afternoons . . .
apart from that 2000-er, nearly all sea and sky, which drove us mad!
Anyway, I thought this one of Westbourne would be a nice present for
your sixtieth, and bring back happy memories.
Lots of love, Jo.
(P.S. We'll see you soon.)

I surveyed the thousand pieces spread over the table. Dear Jo.

It certainly was a lovely idea, but I suspected it would be quite an undertaking!

I turned over the final piece of jigsaw and peered at it.

Surely — yes, with that tiny section of bridge over water it had to be Mill Road.

I decided to make a start, spotting one — or maybe two? — pieces of the old stone bridge.

I'd work outwards from that . . .

The memories were already flooding back. What a wonderful present this was!

An hour later, I had the whole bridge over the river — though it was barely more than a stream, really.

Apart, that is, from the year of the Great Flood.

That year, my dad sandbagged our front door against the terrifying brown torrent, and heaved our precious telly and fridge upstairs with a great deal of bad language.

I had found Lime Avenue, too, with the tiny blob that must have been Mum and Dad's house, where I grew up.

It was then I decided that I should work forward through my life line,

Illustration by Sarah Holliday.

as it were.

I knew it was no use looking for Welford Hospital, of course, with the maternity unit where I was born.

The building had long since been "amalgamated" with the big county hospital.

But at least it meant I could locate the housing estate which now covered the site easily enough.

That was where, in Orchard Close – yes, this must be it – I had lived all my married life.

But this was me rushing on ahead too fast, so . . . where to go next? Our school, of course.

Ah, here it was. Very different from my day, however, for the huge Victorian building which had housed all from infants to seniors, with its high ceilings and echoing corridors, was now one of those trendy, colourful, light-filled boxes.

But here were still the playing fields, where Jo and I froze together playing hockey in navy knickers and Aertex blouses.

That was until the new head of the girls' section heard a group of boys wolf-whistling at us and brought in regulation navy shorts, down to the knee.

I picked up another piece and peered at it.

That patch of green must be St Michael's Park, I thought.

So, yes, this little bit should slot in at one corner, part of the church where I was christened and married and where . . . no, wait, I was getting ahead of myself again.

I put it aside and hunted until I spotted the orderly lines of what had to be the municipal allotments. This was where our dads had grown most of the vegetables we were force-fed "because they were good for us".

Jo and I had had a small square of ground each there, for our houses had no real gardens to speak of, just back yards.

What was it we had grown there?

I remembered nasturtiums, marigolds and love-in-a-mist, and once my gran gave us a packet of scarlet gladioli to share.

Another year we grew monster sunflowers, the seeds supplied by the "Westbourne Herald" in a competition started up to encourage young gardeners.

I smiled to myself as I slotted another piece in, remembering that terrible day when, after a stormy September night, we rushed to the allotments to find those flowers, our pride and joy, prostrate.

We both cried tears of rage.

Of course, all the other entries were also on the ground – except for one boy. Ken Smith's dad was an amateur weather-watcher.

Having had advance warning, Ken had tied his sunflower to their fence.

I can see him now, standing beside his surviving sunflower in the "Herald" the following week, smirking.

Our town was growing up under my fingers.

Another piece just had to be part of the Victorian arcade of shops which led down towards the park.

Even though the streets around it had long since been redeveloped, and some buildings demolished, the arcade was still recognisable, with its stained-glass roof panels and small, gilt domes at either end.

That was where I had got my first job, as a Saturday girl in a trendy hairdresser's. I mostly swept up, but occasionally I was allowed to wash clients' hair before handing them over to Monsieur Paul.

Hmm, yes. Monsieur Paul, the wizard with the scissors, who strangely lapsed from a Parisian accent into broad Yorkshire when the salon closed a few years later.

* * * *

I straightened my back, realising that, without my noticing it, hours had gone by.

By now I'd finished a large part of my old home town, but something was driving me on.

I had to complete this puzzle that made up my life.

Now I was ready to move back to the park. I found a patch of water, which must have been part of the boating lake.

There weren't any boats there any more – something to do with health and safety.

I smiled again, remembering. I'd had my first date on that lake.

It was nearly my last, too, after I almost tipped us in trying to change places with the boy of the hour.

I had decided sitting around was boring, and I wanted to row.

I traced my fingers along the side of the lake until I found what had to be part of the tiny café.

Even on the jigsaw, it looked much fancier than it was in my day, when the grumpy woman who ran it sold only vanilla ice-creams, lollies and sherbet fountains.

The ground there sloped up towards a single tumble-down wall, all that remained of our Norman castle.

One cold winter, the boys made a long slide down the hill which froze harder each day until it gleamed like blue glass.

No girls, not even Jo, who was much more daring than me, would risk it.

It became a badge of honour, however, for the boys to go down it, stay on their feet – and not cry when they broke a wrist or an arm.

It had claimed several victims before Rob Fenton crashed into a tree and was hauled off to hospital with concussion. Workmen came out from the council yards, hacked at it with spades and finally covered it with grit.

Children wouldn't be able to make a slide like that nowadays, I thought. Not with all this global warming.

And, of course, the health and safety issues.

My fingers led me past the castle to find what, almost without thinking, I'd left till last.

Lark Wood, it was called, though to my knowledge larks had never sung there.

It was only a small wood – just a copse, really – but it used to be lovely at all times of the year.

Especially spring, when it was carpeted with bluebells and white wood anemones.

I rested my chin on my hand and gazed down at the jigsaw, seeing through it into the past – my past.

*   *   *   *

It was one day when I'd been picking a bunch of bluebells for Mum. Nowadays that was forbidden, of course, to make sure the flowers lived on until next season and beyond.

It made me a bit sad that youngsters wouldn't know the pleasure of picking bluebells or primroses and burying their noses in the mossy scent of spring.

I was standing there when I saw a young man watching me. As he came nearer, I realised it was Rob.

He was usually to be seen covered in overalls and oil, bending over the ancient Ford Anglia he was doing up as part of his mechanic's apprenticeship.

That day, though, he was smartly dressed in jeans and sweatshirt.

He walked towards me and we gazed at one another. Neither of us spoke a word.

Rain, Rain

RAIN isn't very popular,
But I think that's a shame.
It should be getting wild applause,
Not moans and groans and blame.

It waters plants, it fills the seas,
It helps the rivers run.
It makes gorgeous rainbows
(With assistance from the sun).

But of rain's great advantages
This is the best, by far,
It's been pouring down for hours. Look –
I've got a nice, clean car!

Ewan Smith

It was the strangest thing.
This was the boy I'd known all my life, who had pulled my plaits and dropped my favourite doll in the stream to see if she could swim – she couldn't, as it turned out – and dismantled her pram, assuring me he could put it together again.

Now he was staring at me as though he'd forgotten I was the girl who had tagged after him when he went fishing in that same stream, and who had generally got in his way for years.

He took the bluebells from me, laid them carefully on the ground and kissed me. It seemed as though I'd been waiting all my life for that moment, and just two years later we were married in St Michael's Church.

Mum said we were too young, but Dad disagreed.

"No, our Pat's got a good 'un there."

Jo was my bridesmaid, of course, and I was hers when she married Ken, the Sunflower Champ.

*   *   *   *

I held the final pieces of Lark Wood tightly in my hands.

The real wood was safe for ever now, as it had been handed over to a trust.

iStock.

58

As I sat over the jigsaw I recalled that spring day, almost three years ago, when we stood under the fitful clouds, with birds fluttering in the trees above our heads and a carpet of bluebells and anemones around us.

We'd all gathered there – me, our daughter Katy and her husband Terry – to scatter Rob's ashes in the place where I knew he'd be waiting for me.

* * * *

I was still there, deep in the memory, when my phone rang, making me jump.

"Hello?"

"Hi, Granny."

It was the excited voice of my ten-year-old grandson.

"Oh, hello, love."

"I've done it, Granny! The jigsaw you gave me, I mean."

"Oh, well done, Robbie. And I've just finished mine. Yours was harder, though, with all those tiny pieces of bridge and water."

"So, can we go, Granny? This Saturday, like you promised?"

"We can go on the Cat, walk across the bridge, then have fish and chips in the MCA."

I laughed.

"We certainly can. If your mum says it's all right."

"I've already asked her and she says 'yes'. Brill! Bye, Gran!"

My adorable Robbie rang off.

So that really was something to look forward to.

You might be wondering what Robbie was on about. Go on the Cat for fish and chips?

The Cat is the catamaran that runs downriver to the city.

As for the bridge, well, this one is just a bit bigger than the stone one across the stream in our old park.

The MCA, where Robbie wanted us to have something to eat, is the Museum of Contemporary Art.

It's a stunning building, with its view across the water to the Opera House and the skyscrapers lining the Sydney waterfront.

I've come a long way from my much-loved home town, now laid out before me on the table.

In fact, I doubt if I'll ever go back and see Westbourne in the flesh again.

It was two years ago that I had sat in my back garden under the Bramley apple tree that Rob and I had planted when we were just young parents.

I listened as Katy told me of Terry's plans to join up with an old school friend who'd started a small building company in Sydney.

My darling, considerate daughter had been in tears at the thought of leaving me all alone, for Jo had moved 200 miles away to be near her own son and family.

"I know you love it here, Mum, but would you consider coming out with us?"

Kate's eyes begged me.

I must have hesitated for all of thirty seconds . . .

Now, my nice little bungalow is about a mile away from them, and I've joined a bowls club.

Most days I walk round the park with a few friends from church, where I'm in the choir.

There are none of my beloved bluebells here, of course, but in spring the blossoms of the jacaranda trees have exactly that same heavenly colour.

Terry's business is doing well, Katy has a job in an office in the city, and little Robbie loves it here.

Jo and Ken are coming out to Australia to visit in a couple of months' time, and this Saturday I'm planning to have a lovely day with my grandson.

The next time I complete this jigsaw, I decide, I am going to let Robbie help me.

And while we fit all the pieces together, I can tell him about the town where I grew up, where I met his grandfather, and where his mum was born.

It's important to know these things. ▨

For Tina

by Pamela Wray

Illustration by Jim Dewar.

I FOUND the perfect get-well gift for Tina, my younger sister, in the book aisle of the supermarket. Alongside the usual selection of cookbooks, bestsellers and paperbacks, a new section featured reissued hardback classics, and there I spotted "The Joy Of Ballet" – the book Tina had longed for as a child.

I picked it up, admiring the ethereal, swan-like dancer gracing the cover. But it cost a bit more than I'd brought with me.

My sister's childhood passion had been ballet. But money had been tight at home, and not for buying books about ballet. Especially not for Tina. She was a child trapped in a wheelchair, born with cerebral palsy which had affected her legs. Tina wasn't expected to walk, never mind dance.

I'd heard my parents discussing the book.

"What's the point, love?" Dad had said. "It's expensive, it's too old for her, and it'll constantly remind our poor Tina of something she'll never be able to do."

But Tina could dream, and in her dreams she could dance.

"Last night I danced all night, Beth," she'd say. "It was wonderful."

Back then, I imagined getting that special book for Tina, producing it with a magician's flourish. As she gasped with surprise and delight, I'd lift her up out of her wheelchair and twirl her around.

And for a brief, enchanted time little Tina, light as a snowflake, would point her toes and pirouette like the ballerina on the front of the book.

Sighing for what might have been, I made for the checkout, paid for the shopping in my trolley and packed my bags.

As I left the supermarket, I felt a hand on my arm.

"Just a moment, madam," an ice-cold voice said. "I've reason to believe you've got goods in your bags that you haven't paid for."

I turned to face my accuser. Oh, no! The store detective was Caroline Clements, an old adversary of mine from my schooldays.

One memorable day, Caroline had grabbed Tina's wheelchair in the playground and threatened to tip her over. I'd been on the other side of the playground when the ruckus around the wheelchair alerted me.

"Jeepers, Beth." Tina giggled afterwards. "You raced to my rescue like a red-headed tornado!"

Well, I don't know about that, but I did rush up.

"Don't you dare touch my sister!"

I laid into Caroline, forcing her to let go of Tina's chair, and she backed off, losing face in front of her cronies.

Miss Sharp, the teacher on playground duty, punished the pair of us – we were given a week's worth of detentions, and were both ordered to write 100 lines in our very best script.

Unfair, I thought. I wasn't the one at fault. Caroline was.

But then, I had attacked her.

Now, recognition flashed into Caroline's eyes.

"Well, well. Beth Hunt."

She tightened her grip and frogmarched me towards the manager's office, in full view of shoppers queuing up at the tills.

The manager rose to his feet as Caroline thrust me before him.

"I saw this customer take a book she didn't pay for."

I drew myself up, looked into the manager's face and spoke with all the conviction I could muster.

"Yes, I did pick up a book. I was going to buy it as a get-well gift for my sister. But it was an impulse buy, and when I realised I didn't have enough money with me, I put it back."

"Nevertheless, madam," the manager said, "I'm afraid I must follow company policy and ask you to empty your bags."

Mortified, I unpacked the contents on to his desk. A meal for one; a small loaf; milk, eggs and apples; salad; a carton of orange juice.

When he checked the items against the till receipt, he found I'd taken nothing I hadn't paid for. There was no book.

He apologised for my wrongful detention, looking embarrassed.

"Please take these by way of compensation," he said, offering me a sheaf of money-off vouchers.

Feeling bold, I refused them, and said what I'd really appreciate would be the chance of a job in the store.

"Something clerical," I added hopefully.

I'd had to give up my last job, I explained, as I needed more time to care for my sister after her operation, but she was on the mend now and didn't need as much help.

"Please take the vouchers anyway. We are currently recruiting, so if you e-mail your CV and references to my personal assistant as soon as you get home, and come back here next Monday morning at ten, I'll see what I can do for you."

As I left his office, I heard what he said to Caroline. "You were over-zealous and heavy-handed. Please remember we need to encourage our customers, not send them running to our competitors." I almost felt sorry for her.

* * * *

At Tina's flat, I dumped the bags in the kitchen and popped through to the lounge.

"Hiya. I've got your shopping. I've got these, too." I waved the vouchers. "And I have news."

"You're not the only one with news. I'd better make us a cuppa. This could take a while!"

"Don't worry, I'll make the tea while I put your shopping away."

Returning with a laden tray, I set it down on the coffee table.

"Fire away."

"You first." She laughed. "Before you explode!"

I took a sip of tea and leaned forward.

"You'll never believe what happened."

I told her about Caroline Clements accusing me, and the nice manager, and the chance of a job.

"What a time you've had," she agreed. "But great about the job. Let's hope you get it."

She dunked a gingernut into her tea and grinned.

"Was the manager young and dishy, as well as nice?"

"He was young-ish, and, yes, I suppose he was rather dishy." Blushing, I hurried on.

"Anyway, enough about me. What's your news?"

"Nothing much," she said airily. "Only that I sold a story today."

"Well done, you! A story about dancing?"

"How did you guess?"

We laughed.

"I'm going to treat us to something special with the money I got for it. How about seeing a live performance of our favourite show?"

"'Strictly Come Dancing'? Oh, I couldn't let you."

"I'll not take no for an answer. It'll be my way of saying thank you for all that you do for me. I don't know how I'd cope without you."

I gave her a hug.

"You don't have to cope without me, sis. And you never will."

* * * *

On the morning of my interview, I dressed in a smart skirt-suit, tamed my hair and took extra care with my make-up. After an encouraging grin at myself in the hall mirror, I set off for the supermarket.

At the manager's office, his personal assistant smiled.

"Please go in, Miss Hunt. Mr Parker is expecting you."

The manager rose as I entered.

"Let's begin again, shall we?" he suggested, holding out his hand. "I'm Dan Parker."

"Beth Hunt," I said, shaking his hand.

At the end of the interview, he offered me a place on their training scheme, and said I'd have every opportunity of working my way up in the company – as he himself had done.

He also gave me a voucher towards the cost of the book for Tina.

As I left the store with it in my bag and a smile on my face, I felt a hand on my arm again. Oh, no!

I turned, and sure enough, I came face to face with Caroline.

I felt guilty, even though I hadn't done anything wrong. But then, I hadn't done anything wrong last time, either.

Caroline was smiling hesitantly.

"Beth, I'd like to clear the air between us, if that's OK with you?"

I nodded.

"I'd like that."

"Firstly, I apologise for my treatment of you last time. I'd had a real pig of a day and took it out on you. I was out of order."

"You were doing your job, and it must be difficult."

"But I'm also sorry about that playground incident with your sister. It was an unkind, childish dare. It's preyed on my mind ever since."

"Well, Tina came to no harm, that's the main thing. And I'm sorry I got riled up and hit you so hard I split your lip!"

We grinned at each other. And as we recalled those long, boring detentions under Miss Sharp's beady eyes, doing all those tedious lines, we found we'd arrived at a kind of truce.

*　　*　　*　　*

Later, at Tina's, I produced the book with a magician's flourish, just as I'd longed to do all those years ago.

"Thanks, Beth." Tina smiled. "You shouldn't have."

But her blue eyes danced as she held the book close.

Then, straining with the effort, she pushed herself up from her wheelchair. Leaning laboriously on her crutches, she turned a slow, celebratory twirl.

"Bravo!" I clapped wildly. "You danced a pirouette!"

Tina sat down again abruptly and heavily.

"I wish. But you and I both know I'll only ever dance pirouettes in my dreams." She brightened. "But I've been working hard on my muscle tone and balance, and today at my physio session I did actually walk!"

"Brilliant!" I was overjoyed. "If I'd known earlier, I'd have splashed out on posh chocs for you. Or wine. Why didn't you let me know?"

Tina held up her hands.

"You didn't let me finish. I was going to say that, yes, I did walk a couple of unaided steps today. But they were little wibbly-wobbly, tiptoeing baby steps. Nothing to get excited about."

"Baby steps count."

"Well, it's early days. But I'm hoping that one day I'll walk without crutches, and with you to lend strength to my steps, I might eventually manage a soft-shoe shuffle."

"Of course you will."

"Perhaps we could shuffle to the 'Dance Of The Little Swans' from 'Swan Lake'. A teeny-weeny bit of it, anyhow." Tina laughed and pointed her toes as best she could.

*　*　*　*

On my first lunch break in the supermarket, Caroline waylaid me.

"Tell me to mind my own business if you like, Beth," she said. "But I work out at the leisure centre – I need to keep fit in this job. A new poster caught my eye, for wheelchair dancing. Do you think it'd be something Tina would like to do?"

She produced a flyer.

"There's a contact number, and more info on the website."

"Thanks, Caroline, that was kind of you."

"Search for 'wheelchair dancing' online," she said. "I had a look myself, and there's masses of stuff out there. It's a Paralympic sport now, you know. There are competitions and such like. It's really taking off."

After work I rushed round to Tina's with the flyer, but she was ahead of me. She'd already heard about the class and registered her name.

"Let's face it: I might never dance properly on my own two feet – I'll not stop trying, mind – but this way, I can dance in my chair."

She demonstrated some of the spinning and swivelling movements she'd seen on an online teaching video.

She swung so energetically that she crashed into the furniture and knocked over a china ornament, three houseplants and a table lamp.

"Oh, yeah!" she squealed, uncaring. "Fun! But I'll need more space, or I'll completely wreck the joint!"

"You've made a good start already," I said, gathering up the debris.

*　*　*　*

Classes began in the spring term, on Friday nights at seven p.m. Tina showed me round the mirrored dance studio where they practised.

"There's plenty of room to manoeuvre," she pointed out, giggling about her disastrous attempt at dancing in the flat. "And there's an end-of-term show for families and friends. You'll come, won't you, Beth?"

"Try keeping me away!"

Everyone rallied round for the show. Local shops and businesses provided sponsorship, and the main sponsor was the supermarket – thanks to Dan Parker, who'd shown interest from the start.

He often sought me out in the store and asked about Tina. Naïvely, I fancied he was interested in me, too. I liked him a lot. However, when I asked Caroline if he was unattached, she burst my bubble.

"Dream on, Beth. Others have tried, but it's a waste of time. He's married to the job, and keeps himself to himself."

My hopes and dreams were dashed.

On the night of the show, Tina and the other women dancers wore gorgeous gowns and enviable hair adornments. The men looked debonair in tuxedos with red roses in their buttonholes.

Dan was sitting at the front with the other sponsors when Caroline and I slipped into our seats in the row behind.

He turned and smiled.

With a drum roll, the performance began, and the dancers set the floor alight with their varied and lively routines.

In the final sequence, dry ice transformed the dance floor into a misty lake. To the music of Tchaikovsky, Tina and the other dancers glided gracefully over the surface like skaters dancing in a winter wonderland.

It was magical. I clapped until my hands hurt, tears brimming.

Afterwards, everyone spilled out into the wheelchair-friendly grounds and gathered on the terrace for drinks. Tina, Caroline and I clinked our glasses together and drank to friendship and happy times.

"Right," Tina said. "I'm off to the backstage party now. Don't worry, Beth, I've ordered a cab to take me home.

"As for you two, if you fancy some action there's a smoochy disco in the main hall."

And off she sped, to celebrate her dancing debut with her friends.

A colleague from the store asked Caroline to dance, and they took to the floor.

As I stood there like a wallflower, thinking of sloping off home, Dan appeared from nowhere.

He made a beeline for me, and my thoughts of leaving evaporated. He'd thoroughly enjoyed the show, he said, and what a talented sister I had.

Then he dropped a bombshell. He'd been promoted, and was moving on to a bigger store.

I managed to congratulate him and tried to conceal my disappointment that he was leaving.

I'd always known he was a dedicated manager – "married to the job", as Caroline had said.

Then Dan explained the bigger store was only in the next town, and that he could now ask me out.

"Something I've wanted to do ever since I first met you," he said. "But I couldn't while we both worked in the same branch."

He cleared his throat, seeming shy and uncertain.

"Would you like to go out with me, Beth? I'd really like to get to know you better."

Lost for words, I could only nod and grin.

He smiled.

"Great! How about dinner at Mario's tomorrow night? Do you like Italian food?"

"My favourite."

"Mine, too," he said. "And now, would you like to dance?"

"I'd love to."

We danced together for the rest of the evening, then Dan asked if he could see me safely home.

He kissed me goodnight in the taxi outside my flat.

I danced inside, lighter than air – and I couldn't wait to tell Tina. ∎

Grantham, Lincolnshire

GRANTHAM in Lincolnshire can boast more than its fair share of "firsts". In addition to the UK's first female prime minister, Margaret Thatcher, it was also the workplace of the UK's first female police officer. Edith Smith was appointed to her post in the town in 1914.

The town's most famous son, Isaac Newton, was educated at the King's School in the mid-17th century, before attending Cambridge University. He received the grounding in mathematics that led to him becoming one of the foremost scientists of his age and of history.

A blue plaque on the wall of the old school in Church Street commemorates him. He has also been honoured with a statue in the town, erected in 1858, which stands in front of the town hall. ∎

London Calling

by Maggie Cobbett

L IFE in London isn't all it's cracked up to be, is it?" Claire complained. "A month gone already, and how many people have we met?"

"Outside work, you mean?" Lucy yawned and stretched out her arms so far that they nearly touched both sides of the tiny kitchen. "Well, there's Mrs Johnson . . ."

"Landladies don't count. Anyway, we haven't seen anything of her since we signed the tenancy agreement."

"Her son?"

"Or him, since she sent him to fix the leaky tap."

"The gentleman downstairs, then?"

"Oh, come on, Claire! We only met him when he came up to warn us against holding noisy parties."

"Parties? Chance would be a fine thing. We've got no-one to invite."

"How about some of the other teachers at your school?"

"Oh, they're friendly enough. But most of them rush off to pick up their kids at the end of the day."

"It's the same at the hospital."

Claire sighed.

"Wouldn't it be great to turn back the clock and be students again?"

"Oh, I don't know. We might have had plenty of friends in Leeds, but we were always hard up and . . ."

"Now that we're both qualified and earning decent wages, we don't know anyone."

It was late September, and the walls of the little flat in Bethnal Green – which had delighted the two friends at first – felt as though they were closing in. With their housework done by 10 o'clock and the fridge restocked, the rest of the weekend stretched out before them.

Their personalities were very different. Claire, with her long, fair hair and speedwell-blue eyes, had been the star of the English department's dramatic society, and enjoyed being the centre of attention.

Lucy, whose reddish crop framed a pixie face, had preferred to lend a hand with the costumes – not only because her radiography course allowed little free time.

Illustration by Sarah Holliday.

All the same, the friendship that had begun during Freshers' Week strengthened over the years that followed.

Lucy was the first to be told when Claire was offered the teaching post in London.

It was to Claire that Lucy, eyes red-rimmed and heavy with tears, turned when her medical student boyfriend confessed sheepishly that he'd fallen in love with someone else.

"I can't face running into him every day," she'd wailed. "And that's what would happen at the LGI or St James's."

Given the vastness of Leeds's two great teaching hospitals, that seemed unlikely, but Claire had been quick to seize the opportunity to encourage her friend to move south with her.

Now she was the first to break the glum silence.

"We've got to snap out of this. Didn't Doctor Johnson say that when a man's tired of London, he's tired of life?"

"Of course I'm not tired of London," Lucy retorted, "and I don't suppose you are either, really. It's knowing where to begin that's the problem. The Albert Hall, Big Ben, Covent Garden . . ."

"And then Doctor Johnson's House, if we're going through the alphabet? That's one idea, but I've just had a better one: how about seeing how long it takes us to visit all the properties on the Monopoly board? Let's write down all those we can remember."

"That makes twenty-two streets and four railway stations," Claire announced, some time later. "Quite a challenge! We'll leave out the electric company and the waterworks, because we don't know where they're supposed to be."

Lucy smiled.

"It could still take us until Christmas to get round them all."

"Not necessarily. It depends how much there is to see in each place."

"OK. But we should do them in order. Clockwise round the board."

"Agreed. Come on! Grab your jacket and the guidebook and we'll knock 'em dead in the Old Kent Road!"

* * * *

"It stretches nearly two miles! Do we need to walk the whole length?"

"Only as far as it takes us to find somewhere decent to eat." Claire's stomach had begun to gurgle.

The first property on the Monopoly board, and the only one south of the Thames, had no Underground station. They'd travelled to Elephant and Castle on the Northern Line and walked the rest of the way.

From the junction known as Bricklayers' Arms, in honour of a long-demolished coaching inn, the road ran in a line as straight as when the Romans laid it out as part of their Watling Street.

It was now lined with cosmopolitan shops, cafés and restaurants.

"Have you ever seen such cakes?" Claire sighed as they peered through the door of a busy French bakery. "Why don't we stop here?"

Lucy hesitated.

"We could, but all the inside tables are taken and I don't fancy breathing in traffic fumes while I eat."

"How about buying a few things and finding somewhere for a picnic?"

A few minutes later they were in Burgess Park, threading their way between runners and roller-skaters in search of a vacant bench.

"Please, you may sit here, if you like," a hesitant voice said.

It belonged to a girl with pale blue eyes and long, fair hair.

"Would you like one of these cupcakes?" Claire asked.

"No. I have money, and I am not hungry," was the stiff reply.

"Sorry, I seem to have put my foot in it. I didn't mean to imply . . ."

The girl looked puzzled.

"Put your foot in what?"

Once the misunderstanding was cleared up, they were all laughing.

"Do you work in London?" Lucy asked.

"Yes. I come from Lithuania, work for Mr and Mrs Smith."

"And are you happy there?"

The girl hesitated.

"I have nice room. Good wage . . ." Her voice trailed off. "Too much free time."

"Too much? I don't understand."

"The Smiths are at home at weekends. Like to be with their children. Tell me I can go out."

"Don't they arrange things for you to do?"

"Language classes for foreigners," the girl replied sadly. "I had hoped for English friends, but . . ."

"Well, now you've got some," Claire said stoutly. "We're new here, too, so we know what it's like. Maybe we could exchange numbers?"

"Yes, please!" The girl showed them the phone she had personalised with a little yellow, green and red flag. "My name is Sveta."

"We're Claire and Lucy. Look, we've started to explore London by following the places on a board game we loved as children. I don't suppose you play Monopoly in Lithuania?"

Sveta's eyes sparkled.

"We do. But we go round Vilnius, our own capital city."

*   *   *   *

The girls enjoyed browsing through the colourful goods on offer at the market stalls on Whitechapel Road.

The well-practised patter of the traders was hard to resist, and it wasn't long before Claire was laden with mangoes, a whole pineapple, three bunches of coriander and a huge piece of ginger,

Sveta had bought a fancy scarf to send home to her mother, and Lucy's eye had been taken by some beautiful sequined fabric.

"What a fabulous party dress that would make," she said. "I wonder how much it is?"

"That dark green would certainly suit you, but the price will depend on how much you haggle," a voice in her ear said.

The young man who'd appeared beside her laughed at her surprise. "Haggle?"

"Yes, of course. It's expected. This isn't Liberty's fabric department."

"And you'd know all about that?" Claire snapped.

"Yes, I would, actually. I'm studying fashion at college, and working towards putting on my own show."

"Maybe you could give my friend some advice, then. She's always been handy with a needle."

"Certainly." He turned to Lucy. "Let the fabric do the talking. No fussy details. Something like this, maybe."

Before she could stop him, he'd produced a notebook and pencil from his pocket and was making a rough sketch.

The purchase complete, Lucy turned to say goodbye, but he hadn't finished with her.

"Have you sewn this kind of fabric before?"

She shook her head.

"Well, it isn't cheap, even at the price you've paid, and you don't want to make a mess of it. Before you lay out your pattern pieces, you need to identify the direction of the sequins and make sure that they're all going the same way. Just as you'd look for the nap on a piece of velvet."

"Oh, I know what you mean. I once made that mistake with some evening trousers, and ended up with the legs in different shades."

He laughed.

"It's easily done. Then you'll need extra-sharp point needles for your sewing machine."

"I don't suppose you'd have time to come round to our flat and show her?" Claire asked.

"I'd love to. Give me a ring when you want to get started. My name's Ben, and here's my number."

As Ben disappeared into the crowd, Claire smiled.

"We must go, too, Sveta. I've got marking and lesson prep to do, but tomorrow we can start at King's Cross. Meet us there at eleven?"

*   *   *   *

They found Sveta in the centre of the concourse, eagerly snapping shots of the wave-like steel roof.

"Do you think Queen Boadicea really is buried under here?"

"Who knows? No-one expected to find Richard the Third under a car park in Leicester, so I expect anything's possible."

"If you're done here, I suggest we move on," Claire said. "It's under a mile to the Angel Islington, so we might as well walk."

"That's the only site on our Monopoly board to be named after a building," Lucy explained.

Disappointment awaited. A friendly traffic warden told them that the original inn – and even the Lyons Corner House of the 1920s and 1930s – had been replaced by offices of various sorts.

"However, young ladies," he concluded, "the new Angel over there isn't a bad place to eat."

While they waited for their order to arrive, Claire studied the map.

"It makes more sense to do the next two places in reverse order," she said. "We're close to Pentonville Road, and it would be silly to go all the way down to King's Cross, into Euston Road and then double back."

"Oh, I don't know. Wouldn't that be cheating?"

"Well, Lucy, if it bothers you so much, the last square on that side is the jail. How appropriate!"

"It would be," their waitress said, putting down her heavy tray, "if the prison were actually on Pentonville Road."

"You mean it isn't?"

"No. It's further north, on Caledonian Road. I know that for a fact, because my brother's a prison officer and I volunteer sometimes in the play area for visitors' children."

"What a wonderful thing to do," Lucy said. "I'd love to know more about that."

"I'd be happy to tell you, but not while we're busy. You could meet me back here at the start of my break? My name's Pippa, by the way."

As they were due back at the Angel anyway, after lunch it made sense to cover the sites in the correct order after all.

After Euston Road, Pentonville Road was very busy – even on a Sunday afternoon.

They hadn't covered much of it before the sign over a small red-brick building caught Claire's eye.

"The Poor School? I wonder what that is."

On closer inspection, it turned out to be a drama school.

It was closed that afternoon, but large display boards outside offered a variety of full- and part-time courses, many taking place in the evenings and at weekends.

"Plenty of food for thought there," she said. "Maybe I'll put my name down for something starting after Christmas."

Back at the Angel they found Pippa waiting for them as promised, eager to tell them about her work.

"I don't know if more volunteers are needed at the moment," she concluded, "but let's swap numbers anyway, Lucy, and I can let you know."

* * * *

"We have certainly moved up-market this weekend," Claire commented.

They were standing on the corner of Pall Mall and St James's Street. "All the famous gentlemen's clubs are down here."

"Even the Diogenes," Sveta announced. "The brother of Mr Sherlock Holmes was a member. And Pall Mall was named after an old game like croquet or golf."

"I'm impressed. You've certainly done your homework!"

Lucy glanced at her watch.

"Horse Guards Parade is just behind Whitehall. Anyone fancy seeing the Changing of the Guard?"

It was a unanimous "yes".

The soldiers were a sight to behold, They sat on their immaculately groomed mounts, swords drawn, breastplates shining in the sun.

Afterwards, the girls couldn't resist posing for photographs with an impassive mounted trooper outside.

"I don't think this guy's allowed to crack a smile," a tourist said.

"It's probably more than his job's worth," Claire agreed.

"Well said, madam," a determined-looking young police officer put in. "If it isn't people like that trying to make him laugh, it's young ladies trying to get his telephone number!"

Sveta reddened.

"It must take a lot of training to keep a straight face like that," Claire said, quite unabashed.

"It does. Tradition and discipline are drummed into them from day one. Of course, I can see the attraction," he added ruefully. "They do look very smart in their uniforms."

"So do you. Don't you get any girls' telephone numbers?"

"That would be telling." He grinned.

"I'll bet he could have had yours," Claire whispered to Sveta.

They were almost across to Whitehall when Sveta's phone rang. Something had cropped up, and her employers needed her to look after the children.

"They say to take a taxi," she said. "But where I find one?"

"Ask a policeman!" her friends chorused. "Go on. We'll give you a ring about next weekend."

They'd seen Whitehall so often on screen that they felt as though they knew it already.

They peeped through the gates to see the famous black door of number 10, Downing Street, and then decided that enough was enough for that day.

Retracing their steps, they spotted the same young policeman and were surprised when he beckoned to them and reached into his pocket.

"This belongs to your friend," he said.

In his hand were the mangled remains of a mobile phone, the Lithuanian flag still just about visible.

"Oh, no!" Lucy gasped. "Has Sveta had an accident?"

"No, but this has had it. She was dashing for a taxi when it fell out of her bag. I shouted, but she didn't hear me. By the time I could get across to pick it up, it had been driven over a few times.

"It won't be any good to her, but you're welcome to take it."

"Thank you," Claire said. "But I don't know how we're going to get in touch with her now."

"Maybe she'll contact one of you."

"She can't," Lucy explained. "She put our numbers into her phone, and we don't have a landline. Her employers will, but how many Smiths do you think live in London?"

"Thousands, I imagine. Look, your friend won't know that her phone's smashed up, and she may come back here looking for it.

"Give me a number to pass on if I happen to see her. Charlie Tasker's the name."

*　　*　　*　　*

The following afternoon saw Lucy and Claire heading out up Northumberland Avenue from the Victoria Embankment.

"Sveta would have loved this," Lucy said. "According to the guidebook, Arthur Conan Doyle mentioned its hotels several times."

"If we turn off into Northumberland Street, we can visit the Sherlock Holmes. Apparently it's full of themed items."

The head of the Hound of the Baskervilles leered down at them from its glass case as Damien, the chatty young waiter, mentioned that he was just "resting" between acting jobs.

Claire took the opportunity when he brought the bill to ask his opinion of the Poor School.

"Excellent," he said. "I studied there myself. Look, I can't talk now, but give me a ring some time and I'll be happy to tell you all about it."

He scribbled down his number for her and dashed off.

"It's amazing how many people we've met since we began this challenge," Lucy commented as they arrived back at their flat.

Claire's phone rang. It was PC Charlie Tasker.

"Guess who I've got here with me," he said.

Claire put her phone on speaker and they could hear Sveta giggling happily in the background.

*　　*　　*　　*

Later that month, Claire and Lucy invited all their new friends to join them in their flat. It wasn't exactly a dinner party, because there wasn't room for everyone around the table, although they did have plenty of food.

It wasn't rowdy either, much to the relief of their downstairs neighbour.

Sveta and Charlie arrived first, hand in hand. They were followed by Pippa and her brother, actor Damien and Ben.

"Actually," Claire whispered to Lucy when they met in the kitchen, "I think Pippa's got her eye on Damien."

"And her brother's got his on you."

"And to think that we haven't even made it halfway round the Monopoly board yet!" ∎

Magical Olympic Moments

1984

As soon as the first few notes of Ravel's "Bolero" are played, most of us think of ice-skaters Torvill and Dean and their success at the 1984 Winter Olympics in Sarajevo. The duo scooped gold after a dazzling performance which began with the competitors on their knees.

Their iconic musical choice was a bit different from the normal. Jayne Torvill and Christopher Dean had three world championships under their belts, so they had the confidence to dare to be different when they took to the ice. They only had four minutes to perform, but needed 4.28 for "Bolero"; hence the kneeling pose since the stopwatch only started once the skaters' blades touched the ice.

The overall effect brought goose-bumps to all those watching – and it had nothing to do with the chilliness of the ice arena. All nine judges awarded an unprecedented perfect score of 6.0, and life for the insurance clerk and the policeman would never be the same again. ■

Alamy.

A Lesson Learned

by Pamela Ormondroyd

URTHERMORE, I will not tolerate seeing berets worn at the back of heads with the badge unseen. You should be proud of our school. Now, go to your lessons and do not incur my wrath again."

"Yes, Miss Hartson. Sorry, Miss Hartson."

Sally Lawson and Melanie Fitch, duly admonished, eyed each other with a mischievous glance as they hurried off to their history lesson, while Miss Hartson tut-tutted her way back to her study.

At the end of the corridor a smiling Miss Sibley peered out of her empty art room. Those sixth-form girls might be nearly eighteen years old, but no student was ever too old to avoid a dressing-down whilst in the care of Miss Hartson, headmistress of the prestigious Barley High School for Girls.

Iris Sibley did feel a little compassion for them, however, for in a few months' time, once the summer term had ended, all these girls would be independent young women, off to various colleges and corners of the country. A little tolerance of their individuality couldn't do any harm, surely?

Besides, having to wear a beret on top of the latest beehive style would be enough to crush anyone's spirit, especially after the daily morning ritual of back-combing, styling and spraying.

The double doors opened with a jolt at the farthest end of the long corridor as the fifth-formers made their way down to the art room. Iris darted back and prepared herself for an hour-long session of still life.

$*$ $*$ $*$ $*$

"It's getting beyond a joke," Vera Hartson said as the staff convened for their morning break. "Skirts are getting shorter, hair is getting higher. We simply must get on top of it. I had to reprimand Sally Lawson and Melanie again this morning.

"They should know better. The younger girls look up to them, so they should be setting an example."

"Don't you think you might afford the sixth form just a little slack,

Illustration by iStock.

Miss Hartson?" Iris suggested. "I mean, they're practically adults now and will be leaving us soon."

Miss Hartson shook her head. If all her teachers were like Miss Sibley she would have anarchy on her hands!

"Once you start making concessions, you find boundaries are pushed even further, Miss Sibley. Here at Barley High we have traditions and standards to maintain. I thought you would be aware of this already, having been with us for two years."

Iris took a deep breath and gritted her teeth. She would have liked to have argued her corner with Vera Hartson, but not in front of all the other staff, most of whom were a lot older than herself.

She had tried it a few times before and received only a sharp rebuff from her superior.

"I don't understand why Sally's parents are so keen for her to go to drama school," Vera Hartson continued. "There's no future or security in acting. And Melanie Fitch was an excellent science prospect until she decided she wanted to become an impoverished artist.

"No disrespect to you, Miss Sibley, for of course I know that some girls may be especially gifted in the arts. But when one is academically inclined and smart, like Melanie, it seems such a waste of seven years' education not to have higher aspirations."

Iris winced again, but hid her displeasure by reaching for a newspaper.

* * * *

"Oh, Miss Sibley, guess what we've got?"

Iris was just crossing the playground one calm, sunny morning when Sally Lawson and her friend, Melanie, came running over to greet her.

Iris stopped and waited for them.

"Tickets for the Beatles!" Sally said breathlessly. "My dad bought one each for me and Mel to go to their show at the Regal a week on Friday."

"Isn't it a great eighteenth-birthday present, miss?" Melanie triumphantly waved her ticket about. "They're like gold dust, you know. People have been queuing for days for one of these, but Sal's dad delivers stuff to the theatre so he managed to get two."

Iris smiled at the excitement of the pair – Sally with her red hair and freckles and Melanie with her bright blue eyes and kiss curls. They were like a breath of fresh air, and as she watched them catch up with other girls to reveal their spoils, Iris knew she would miss them when they left school.

In some ways, they reminded her of herself at the same age: full of optimism, hopes and dreams for the future.

As she strode along the corridor to prepare the art room for the morning's first lesson, Iris's mind drifted back to the summer of 1945, the last year of the war, when Bill, one of the farmhands, had run across the meadow of Langley's Farm waving a newspaper in his hand and yelling excitedly at the top of his voice.

All the land-girls, including Iris, had stopped in their tracks, wondering what had happened. But the news was good. The war was practically over and very soon all the troops would be returning home.

Mr Langley, the farmer, had ordered work to stop early that day so that they could all have a bit of a celebration.

It was while walking along the brook later, with the realisation that he might never see her again, that Bill had found the courage to propose. And when Iris had said yes there had been even more celebrating on the farm that night.

Iris looked out of the large picture window and over the rooftops to the countryside beyond. She would have enjoyed being married to a farmer. She would have helped willingly with the lambing and milking and would have been in her element sitting out in the fields with her easel and paint palette in her free time.

But it hadn't worked out like that. Her parents were horrified at the thought of their only daughter getting married to a man she hardly knew. She was only eighteen, they said, a mere child, and couldn't possibly know what love was. Then they bundled her off to a relative in London in a flurry of deception.

Iris often thought about Bill, wondering what had happened to him.

"Can we go outside to sketch today, Miss Sibley?"

"Please, miss, it's such a lovely day."

Iris was roused from her thoughts by a group of first-formers.

"Good idea, girls," she said, smiling. "Let's do that."

*　　*　　*　　*

A week later, Iris was on her way to the school foyer to collect her post when she saw Sally and Melanie standing dejectedly outside Miss Hartson's study.

"Oh, no, girls. Not more trouble?"

"We were whispering in assembly," Melanie admitted. "It wasn't really our fault."

"A girl was telling us the Beatles had just got to number one with 'Please, Please Me' and I let out a little squeal."

"Let me guess. Miss Hartson heard you and wasn't too pleased with you at all!"

Iris had, in fact, heard the group play on the radio one weekend and had found her feet tapping to the catchy beat. She could understand why the Fab Four were becoming so popular with the youngsters.

"So, what's happened?"

"Miss Hartson's given us both a double detention for next Friday, the day we were going to the Beatles show, Miss Sibley," Sally said, looking very down in the mouth.

"Oh."

"We've been trying to work out if we'd have time to get to the theatre for the six o'clock start, but there's no way we'd do it, not with a double detention," Melanie continued. "We begged Miss Hartson to let us do the detention another night, but she said definitely not, and that this might just be the lesson we needed to behave more responsibly in future."

There was a pause as Iris shook her head.

"Could you have a word with Miss Hartson, Miss Sibley?" Sally begged. "I'd volunteer to do litter-picking duties for a month if we can change the day."

"We're not trying to get out of it altogether, miss," Melanie added. "We just want to defer it."

"Well, I don't know," Iris said, feeling a little pressurised. "I mean, you've both had warnings. You know the rules."

Then the bell went for start of lessons and Iris watched as the two teenagers dawdled miserably down the corridor.

*　　*　　*　　*

"Are you busy, Miss Hartson?"

It was the end of a humid, sultry afternoon as Iris peered round the door of the headmistress's study. Vera Hartson looked up from her desk where she was reading.

"I wonder if I might have a word?"

Vera removed her glasses and ushered Iris in.

"Yes, of course," she said. "Take a seat."

"I just wanted to ask if you might reconsider the double detention you've given Sally Lawson and Melanie Fitch," Iris began. "It's Sally's birthday next weekend, you see, and she and Melanie were so looking forward to seeing a special show. It's been planned for some time."

Vera left her chair and walked slowly over to the window. A pretty pink rose bush in the outside garden swayed gently against the sill.

"I'm afraid, Miss Sibley, that you sometimes display a vulnerability which certain younger members of our establishment seek to exploit. They are just schoolchildren, after all, and while they are here they simply cannot be allowed to dictate the rules to suit. A detention is meant to be punitive so that a lesson is learned."

"But don't you think that, on this occasion, you may have been a little harsh, Miss Hartson?"

Vera Hartson spun round and glared.

"I have been headmistress of this school for the past twelve years and under my administration the school has become one of the best in the county. Are you questioning my authority, Miss Sibley?

"I suppose if it were left to so-called 'forward' thinkers such as yourself, the girls would be allowed to dress and do as they wished. The Swinging Sixties syndrome may be taking over cities like London and Liverpool, but I will never allow it to penetrate the walls of Barley High."

"But surely we ought to be preparing our girls for the modern world, Miss Hartson? That's a part of our job here, isn't it? They should be permitted now and again to express themselves, to put an opinion forward."

Miss Hartson sighed and sat down again at her desk. She looked across at Iris with a scowl as if the young teacher were one of her errant pupils.

"This establishment is no place for liberal thinking while I am in charge," she said. "And if I were you, Miss Sibley, I would seriously question whether I really should be working in a place of such high prestige and long traditions."

Iris was incensed. All she had come for was to ask for a small reprieve for two of her pupils; just a little reasoned flexibility. Now her whole teaching ethos was being questioned!

"Actually, I have already been considering my position here," she said, rising quickly and knocking the desk with her knee. "I'm sorry we do not see eye to eye, Miss Hartson. I have a great affection for the school, but I think it is best for both of us that I leave at the end of term. I shall write my letter of resignation this evening."

Iris then walked briskly out of the room and hurried down the front steps and across the yard.

✳   ✳   ✳   ✳

Miss Hartson watched her go and immediately regretted the tough stance she had taken.

She knew she was harsh sometimes, but it was her way. And it was a way that had always worked for her in the past.

In some respects, she envied young Miss Sibley. She was a good teacher and had an easy manner with the girls, and it was obvious they all liked and respected her for it. She would be missed.

*   *   *   *

It wasn't too difficult for Iris to get another job interview. She had a friend at the technical college in the next town, Fordbridge, and knew they were already interviewing for an art teacher for the autumn term.

It took just one quick phone call and she was offered an interview within two days. Her qualifications were particularly good and the fact that she was already working at Barley High was a recommendation in itself.

Iris was well acquainted with Fordbridge since it was in the countryside around the little river valley town where she had once worked as a land-girl. It was also the home town of her darling Bill, although she knew he had left it a short time after their thwarted romance.

The interview went well. They would let her know within a week, they said. The college was modern and the students seemed bright and enthusiastic.

Iris smiled to herself as she crossed over to the main gate, though. Leather jeans, starched petticoats, white lipstick and masses of popper beads would have been an absolute no-no in Vera Hartson's eyes!

A chap with greying hair came round the corner of the building carrying a ladder and she had to stand back to let him past. As she did so, Iris let out a gasp, recognising him.

It was Bill. Older, of course, but still handsome and obviously still healthy and fit.

She watched as he placed the ladder against one of the college walls, climbed up halfway and proceeded to work on one of the window frames.

Iris couldn't speak and seemed rooted to the spot.

After 19 years, Bill was back in Fordbridge. He'd returned to his roots. Had he come back hoping he might see her again?

Her heart leaped. She had never forgotten him.

She vaguely recalled the dark days in London as she'd desperately written letter after letter to Langley's Farm in the hope that Bill would understand what had happened. That he might come up to the city and rescue her. But her letters had been returned unopened. No-one knew where he was.

She thought of the college her parents had enrolled her at and the horrid month she had spent in typing lessons. Then a faint smile touched her lips as she recalled how she'd walked out one day and found a place at art school, where she felt immediately at home and mixed with the arty bohemian set whom her parents would have hated.

She'd had a few short-lived romances over the years, of course. She was a pretty girl, after all. But Bill had always been on her mind. No young man had made her feel the same way as her Bill . . .

Suddenly a young lad of about fifteen ran across the yard and stopped and looked up the ladder.

"Hey, Dad, will you be home for tea? Fish and chips tonight, don't forget."

Bill looked down and grinned.

"Yes, I'll be there, son," he called down. "Put mine in the oven, though, just in case."

Reality clicked in. So, they had both moved on – Iris with her career and Bill with a family.

He had fallen in love again and this time, for him, it seemed it had lasted.

Iris put down her head and hurried by, leaving the past behind.

* * * *

The job offer came a few days later, though it didn't seem so important to her now.

Back at Barley High and rooting through the stock cupboard and finding paintings from years before, Iris realised just how much she loved the old school.

She began to think she had been a little hasty in handing in her resignation. Miss Hartson's views might be a tad old-fashioned, but she did have the best interests of the girls at heart.

Iris made up her mind to apologise and see if she could possibly withdraw her notice.

As she searched through the folder of Melanie's artwork, she was surprised at how prolific the girl's work output had been.

Melanie had a real talent and an eye for colour and perspective. She would do well at art college.

Iris lifted up a large canvas that had been placed beneath the folder and held it up. She took it across to the light and admired it with a gasp of delight.

It was a wonderful painting of Barley High on a summer's day. Girls were outside on the grass, walking, talking and reading, while the school building, in all its Victorian glory, sat proudly in the background.

As the girls filed out of the classroom after the afternoon session, Iris caught up with Melanie and Sally as they headed for the gym.

"It's a wonderful painting, Melanie!" she said. "I don't know why you haven't shown it to me before. It's painted with real joy and affection for the old place."

"Well, I have got a soft spot for the old school," Melanie replied with a smile. "I know Sal and I haven't been ideally behaved pupils, but we've loved being here. And even though I'm still cross about the detentions, I'll be really tearful when I leave."

"And me," Sally agreed. "I'll be sorry to say goodbye to Miss Hartson, too. We know she only really wants the best for us, and I'm sure her love of literature inspired me to want to be an actress. I mean, look how dramatic and over the top she is herself at times!"

Iris smiled and nodded. The views of the two girls had reinforced her own thoughts.

She must go and see Miss Hartson and clear the air.

* * * *

"Come in."

Miss Hartson looked up and there was a hint of a smile on her lips.

"More pleas on behalf of current mischief makers, Miss Sibley?"

"No." Iris returned the smile, while Miss Hartson ushered her to take a seat.

"I've come to apologise for the other day, actually, Miss Hartson. I was out of order and I didn't mean to challenge your authority."

Miss Hartson was quiet for a few moments, then she spoke with a quiet voice.

"You weren't completely out of order, my dear," she said. "In fact, I've had time to mull over what you said and really you were quite right when you hinted I hadn't moved with the times.

"I know it's a different world today and changing rapidly all the time, but it's very difficult for an 'old school' type like me to adapt, to soften my approach without fear of losing face.

"I do care about the charges in my care. Very much. They are like a family to me in a way. But, yes I am probably sometimes overly hard on them, and I do agree that sixth formers are much more mature these days and need a more flexible, modern approach.

"Maybe employing a teacher with special duties in this field would be a good idea."

Iris sat up in her chair. Miss Hartson's change of attitude had taken her by surprise.

"The teacher who replaces me?" she stammered.

"Or the teacher who is sitting in front of me right now."

"But I gave in my resignation, and –"

"Really? I don't seem to remember any resignation. Oh, dear, you don't think I threw it out with the rubbish, do you?"

Iris laughed then and even Miss Hartson chuckled.

"I'd be flattered," Iris said. "Now, I wonder if you'd come down to the art room tomorrow, Miss Hartson. I've something rather special to show you."

* * * *

The next day, Miss Hartson could barely take her eyes off Melanie's grand portrayal of Barley High. Iris had mounted the picture on a wall in the art room and the headmistress loved the picture so much that she asked if it might be displayed in the school foyer so that all visitors to the school could see it.

Then she informed Melanie and Sally that she had decided to defer their detention to another date, so that they could go to the Beatles concert, after all.

The mood in the school felt lighter already, Iris thought as she prepared her bag to go home.

Then, as she glanced fleetingly out of the classroom window, she saw a man waiting at the gates. She took a huge intake of breath, for she recognised Bill again.

What was he doing here? Did he have another child, a girl at Barley High that she didn't know about?

There was only one way to find out.

She ran down the corridor and across the yard, then stopped about five yards away from the man she had loved for so long.

"It is you, isn't it?" he said. "I saw you at the college and recognised you at once, but you hurried off before I had a chance to speak to you."

"But how did you find me?"

"I went into the college office and they told me you'd been for an interview and that you worked here. I had to see you."

Iris didn't know if she could bear hearing about his present life, about his son and his wife, and to discover that he could now never be hers.

Was that why he had come? To tell her he'd found happiness in spite of her?

"I knew you'd been sent to London after the war, but there was no way I could ever have hoped to find you there. I upped sticks and went down south. I had a brother there, and after the war we set up a building business. It worked out well, but I always knew I'd come back to Fordbridge one day."

"You have a son. I saw him at the college."

"Yes, I have a son." Bill smiled. "He's a smashing lad. After his mum died, he and I . . ."

"You were married and she died?"

Iris moved closer.

"Yes, Tom was eighteen months old. It was hard at first but we gradually got through it. We've been on our own since, the two of us."

"Oh, Bill, I'm so sorry. If only I'd known . . ."

He held out his arms and she ran towards him.

"I've so much to tell you. Such a lot to explain," she said.

"All in good time, eh?" he replied.

She nodded and slipped her arm through his as they walked slowly along the road towards the town.

*   *   *   *

Miss Hartson watched from her study window and smiled. No-one was too old to learn a life lesson, to move forward and make things right.

Not even her.

Something caught her eye and she looked down at the bicycle shed, to see one of the fifth formers stuffing her beret inside her satchel before she went home.

Miss Hartson lifted up the sash window and roared, making the girl jump.

"Put that beret back on your head, pronto! Be proud, walk tall and show that badge to the world. You're a Barley High girl, after all!" ■

Loch Fyne from Hell's Glen, Argyll and Bute.

LOCH FYNE is a sea loch forming part of the coast on the Cowal Peninsula on the west coast of Scotland. It is the longest sea loch in the country, having a length of around 40 miles from Inveraray to the Kyles of Bute. Its name means "loch of the vine" (or "wine"), though there is not thought to be any connection with wine-making in the area.

It is, however, well known for its oysters. Tourists also visit to enjoy the spectacular scenery and wildlife. On land, deer and red squirrels are plentiful. In the air, buzzards and both native species of eagle – the golden eagle and the sea eagle – abound. Glancing seawards, you might be lucky enough to spot otters or dolphins. ■

The Corncochle Tree

by Moira Gee

GRAN looked disappointed.

"I was sure it was along this part of the road. I know it was at the top of a hill because my dad used to keep encouraging me. 'Come on, Nellie, see if you can cycle a bit further this time.'

"And every time, he'd remind me I'd be all right once I got to the Corncochle Tree. 'It's downhill from there so we can freewheel'."

Chrissie pictured her gran as a girl, aged ten or eleven, out for a run with her dad, cycling around the Lanarkshire countryside. They'd pass through villages, waving to friends and stopping to eat their sandwiches beside a burn.

Chrissie loved when Gran told her stories of her childhood, and about all the mischief she and her friends used to get up to. They'd seemed to have such a lot of fun, despite the austerity of the time.

It was easy to see that Gran had been brought up during the war by the way she never threw anything away.

"I was sure we were on the right road," she was saying now. "I did love the Corncochle Tree. Perhaps my memory's playing tricks on me."

She chuckled, but there was a wistful look in her eye and Chrissie felt her heart twist, wishing there was a tactful way to say what she was thinking.

"The tree might not be there any more, Gran. It was a long time ago."

"Over seventy years." Gran nodded in agreement. "Ah, well, we've seen a lot of other things these past couple of days, haven't we?"

Chrissie smiled.

"We certainly have. It's been lovely."

Chrissie wasn't entirely sure what had prompted her to suggest taking her grandmother away for this weekend trip.

Perhaps it was seeing the number of photos in Gran's living-room increasing – babies, first days at school, graduations and wedding photos. Her cousin's wife had just had a baby girl, another had got engaged, and another was expecting her second baby soon.

They were all there on Gran's walls, on display cabinets, on top of the television; a lifetime of lives, passing before her eyes.

Gran interrupted her thoughts.

"It's a pity about the tree, but remember I pointed out my uncle's old shop back along the road? It's a tearoom now. Shall we pop in?"

Chrissie noticed that Gran shivered a little as she spoke, so she turned the car round and headed back towards the warmth of the tearoom.

Gran was thrilled to be inside the old house again, and soon struck up a conversation with the present owner, who pointed out an old photo of the building back in the Forties. Chrissie watched the pleasure on her gran's face as she chatted and shared reminiscences with the lady.

"This part was the living-room, and my brother and I used to play in the corner over there. My uncle had a box of tin soldiers and my aunt let me dress up her old dolls. China ones, they were, really fragile.

"The adults all sat around the room. Sometimes the men would play cards – my mother always disapproved, especially if it was a Sunday. The women usually had knitting or darning to do. But we always had a good feed at Auntie Bessie's."

As they enjoyed tea and cakes they looked through the photos on Chrissie's camera, where she'd captured all the places they'd visited.

Their first port of call had been the house by the station at Leadhills, where Chrissie learned that her great-great-grandfather had been stationmaster.

"My dad was born in that bedroom up at the top."

There had followed all sorts of little personal landmarks.

"Here's where my dad was kicked by a donkey when he was eleven. He had a scar on his head for the rest of his life. This is the church he used to go to . . ."

After Leadhills they'd visited the village of Brocketsbrae.

"It was so strange to see the house where my mother was born. I could have sworn that whitewashed wall at the front was a huge thing. I seem to remember it towering over me."

Gran laughed when she saw the two-feet-high wall, too low for her to sit on to have her photo taken beside her grandparents' house.

"This was Mum's school. She was a nurse in Stonehouse Hospital in the war. I had to put the dinner on if she was on a back shift. I used to get into trouble because I'd forget to put the tatties on in time . . ."

Chrissie laughed. She always found herself laughing at Gran's tales – she could even make a scolding sound funny.

"Thank you for this trip, Chrissie. It was lovely to see those old places again. It's amazing how many are still standing after all this time."

"I've enjoyed it, too. Uncle Alan's looked up his side of the family tree, but I didn't know anything about your side. It's been lovely.

"You seemed to have a lot of fun when you were a child," Chrissie went on. "It's strange to say that, with the war and everything."

"Of course, it was a terrible time, but there was a great community spirit. Even after the war we were rationed. That went on for years. But it was a good life. Me and my pals were always getting up to something."

Clearly, Gran had been a real livewire in her younger days. Actually, Chrissie thought, she still was!

It was just after they'd ordered their second pot of tea that Gran leaned forward and spoke more seriously.

"So, what about you, my dear? Is there something on your mind?"

The sudden change of subject took Chrissie by surprise.

"Me? What do you mean?"

"You seem distracted," Gran said.

Chrissie looked up into her grandmother's wise and loving face and smiled. She'd always been an astute character.

"Is it your job? Are you still enjoying it?"

"I'm not sure if 'enjoying' is the right word." Chrissie hesitated. "I wish I could do more. I suppose I don't find it fulfilling."

"I remember when you started, you were so excited to be showing people round new homes, starting new lives."

"I was, wasn't I?"

Chrissie smiled at the memory of her younger self, so keen to be starting out in her first job in an estate agent's office.

"But it's not enough for me now."

"Could you look for another job, more in line with what interests you?"

"That's the thing, I am still interested in houses, but whenever I'm showing people round, I find myself looking at the decor more and more. I think I'm more interested in design and decorating, that sort of thing."

"Yes, you were always good at art, weren't you?" Gran nodded, helping herself to another biscuit.

"The thing is, it's tricky to give up work and go to college once you get used to the money, and I'm still paying off my car. So I've been looking at different courses – online, or evenings at college."

"That's a good idea. Tricky doesn't mean impossible." Gran smiled encouragingly. "And you're still young. Twenty-three, aren't you?"

"Next month."

"Well, then, you've plenty of time. You might change your mind fifty times before you get to my age! As long as you keep aiming for the life you want, no matter how many twists and turns the road takes, you'll be like me when I reached the Corncochle Tree.

"You can freewheel once you've done the hard work and enjoy the rewards."

Chrissie nodded thoughtfully, stirring her tea.

"Were you happy with the choices you made in your life, Gran?"

"In my day we didn't have as many choices as young people do nowadays, but yes, on the whole, I've been happy with my life."

Gran looked keenly at the troubled young face opposite hers.

"I'm guessing it's not just your job that's troubling you. Is there something else on your mind?"

Chrissie gave a quiet sigh.

"It's Declan."

"What about him?"

The lack of surprise in Gran's voice made Chrissie feel rather sheepish.

"He went for an interview last week in Dublin. It's for a really good job, and he's always talked about going back to his 'Old Country'. I can understand that – all his family are there, and his old friends."

"Has he asked you to go with him?"

"Sort of. He hasn't really asked, but I think he kind of assumes we're together for ever and . . . and I'm just not sure we are."

"What makes you feel that way? I thought the two of you were happy."

"We were. We are. He's nice and funny and kind, and we have a lot in common." Chrissie hesitated. "But what about *my* family? All *my* friends? I've grown up here. My life's here. I'd be giving it all up."

Gran considered for a moment.

"Perhaps your answer is in where you said 'but'."

"What do you mean?"

"You listed all the good things about Declan – nice, funny, things in common, and then came the 'but'. Maybe the 'but' is more significant than the situation."

"What do you mean?"

"I can only speak for myself, but when your grandpa asked me to marry him and move to Kent, it was the other way around. I had a life here, a job, a family, my friends, the community, my hobbies, but . . ."

"What was the 'but' in your case?"

Gran's smile was wistful.

"But I loved him," she said quietly. "I didn't feel as if I was giving up my own life. He was my life. We made a life together."

"I don't remember Grandpa very well, but you seem to have such happy memories of him."

"Of course I do. I'm not saying it was all plain sailing, but yes, we were happy. Your grandpa was the cousin of our neighbours and used to come up nearly every year. After we married, I moved down to Maidstone with him because he had a job there.

"It was different in those days, of course. But I wanted to go. It was only after we had the family that we decided to move back up here."

She smiled.

"We had three lovely children. Then, when they grew up and married, we had all you grandchildren to enjoy."

She laughed.

"And now, of course, they're starting their own families, so it's all beginning again. I can hardly keep up with them all!"

Gran looked again at the old photograph on the wall.

"It's nice to look back. Once you get to my age there's more behind you than in front of you." Gran smiled wryly. "But you've got a whole life to look forward to. And that might be in Dublin, with Declan."

"What if it doesn't work out?"

"Then you come back – or go somewhere else."

"You make it sound simple." Chrissie smiled weakly.

"Not necessarily simple. But you make the rules of your life and if it doesn't feel right then change it. A job, a relationship, where you live . . . it's your decision. I chose what I wanted to do."

Gran paused and contemplated the plate of cakes in front of them.

"You know, I'm still on holiday. I think I want another cake."

She winked at her granddaughter.

"Do you know what you want, Chrissie?"

$$* \quad * \quad * \quad *$$

Back at their hotel that night, after Gran had gone to bed, Chrissie sat in her room thinking. At last, she picked up her phone.

Declan was surprised to hear from her.

"Hi, beautiful, I didn't expect you to phone."

"Yes, I wasn't sure where we'd be or if I'd have time. But Gran's gone to bed early. I think she's worn out." She forced a laugh.

He chuckled.

"Is she enjoying herself? Are you having a good time?"

"It's lovely. I'm learning a lot about Gran's family – my family. She's happy seeing all her old haunts. You know, her home."

There was an uneasy pause. Taking a breath, Chrissie decided it was time to bite the bullet.

"Talking of home, have you heard from Ireland?"

He hesitated.

"Yes."

"And?" But Chrissie knew what he was going to say.

"I didn't want to tell you over the phone."

"It's OK, Declan. You might as well tell me. What did they say?"

"The job's mine if I want it."

Chrissie could hear the suppressed glee in his voice. She swallowed.

"That's great, Declan."

"I asked for a couple of days to think about it."

She was surprised.

"Do you have to think about it?"

"No, but you do." She heard him take a breath. "Chrissie, if you're not sure about coming with me, or if you don't want me to take it . . ."

"What? No, Declan, you have to take it. It's what you want, isn't it?"

"It's a really good position and I'd be good at it." He paused. "But it's more than that, Chrissie. It's –"

"Home," she finished for him. "Declan, I want you to take the job. You'd regret it if you didn't." Chrissie felt her voice falter. "But I won't be coming with you."

"Chrissie!"

"No, Declan, you've found your dream job and you'll be great at it."

"What about you?" He sounded sad.

"I need to find what I really want to do with my life."

She took a deep breath.

"All I know is I don't want to leave Scotland. This is my home."

"I see."

"Good luck, Declan."

"You, too."

When Chrissie hung up, she was surprised to realise that her heart wasn't broken. She knew she'd miss Declan. He'd been a part of her life for a long time. But that shouldn't be her only reason to stay with him.

It was time to live the life she wanted. All she had to do was decide which direction she wanted to take now.

As Gran said, there would be many roads to travel and a lot of exciting things to discover along the way.

She clicked open her laptop and was about to look up jobs when she paused. There was no need to hurry.

She was still on holiday. Job-hunting could wait.

Instead, she typed *Corncochle Tree*.

＊　＊　＊　＊

"Agrostemma githago," Chrissie read from her phone. "Pink family. Silky annual or biennial. Lance-shaped leaves. Noxious weed of grain fields, waste places.

"Corncockle or corncochle. Once believed to be extinct due to modern farming methods. Tall magenta-purple blooms; slender hairy stems."

Gran looked puzzled and a little sad.

"So it's not a tree? That's so strange. Dad always said 'the Corncochle Tree'. It's not a name you'd make up."

"Maybe the flowers grew round the bottom of the tree," Chrissie said. "Or even on it, hanging from the branches like mistletoe does."

"Or perhaps it was a grain field. It says it grows in grain, doesn't it?" Gran mused. "The tree might have been in the corner of a wheat field."

"That could have been it," Chrissie agreed.

"Well, maybe it's time we set off. You've a long drive ahead of you."

As they collected their belongings from their rooms and handed in their keys at reception, Chrissie was aware of a heaviness in her heart.

It was a lost feeling which had nothing to do with Declan. It was more a sense of unfinished business, as if something were missing.

She closed the boot on their bags and stood watching Gran for a moment.

She smiled affectionately as Gran settled herself in the front passenger seat, placing her bag at her feet and fastening her seatbelt.

It had been a special weekend with lots of happy memories and funny stories. There had been poignancy in the trip, but Gran was always such good company, with her sense of humour and her love of having fun.

She had a talent for finding something special in the smallest occasion, an adventure in the shortest of journeys.

Chrissie opened her door and climbed into the driver's seat.

"Is there anywhere else you'd like to see? We're in no hurry."

She knew she was playing for time. She wanted an excuse to prolong this special time, unwilling for it to come to an end.

Gran looked doubtful.

"It's a long drive back to Montrose. Won't Declan be expecting to see you this evening?"

"No, Gran, he isn't expecting to see me."

"I see. Are you all right?" Gran asked gently.

"Yes, I'm fine. Really." Chrissie meant it. "Come on, let's get going."

"I'm sorry things haven't worked out for the two of you, but you mustn't regret what you've done." Gran gave her hand a squeeze. "As you get older, you don't regret the things you did so much as the things you didn't do."

Her mind suddenly made up, Chrissie turned the key in the ignition.

"You're right, Gran, as usual. So I think we should have one last look for the Corncochle Tree."

It was a quiet road, so Chrissie was able to drive at a leisurely pace, giving Gran time to study their surroundings.

"This bend in the road looks familiar – yes, this is more like it. We must have turned back too soon last night."

"Shall we take a walk along?" Chrissie suggested. "It can't be far."

She was reluctant to raise Gran's hopes, but the older lady had her seatbelt off and was opening the door as soon as the engine stopped.

She trotted off at a brisk pace and Chrissie grinned as she locked the car and hurried to catch up with her.

"I think there was a farmhouse down in that dip. You could see it from the top of the hill here. Yes, look!" She pointed in triumph.

Chrissie saw the sprawling building nestling at the foot of the hills. It looked tired but comfortable, reminding her in a strange way of Gran.

Not that she looked tired just now. Gran's eyes were shining as she kept walking, excitement giving strength to her slight frame.

"The tree was at the edge of a field, just inside a wall or a fence, I'm sure. It was definitely at the top of a hill."

Chrissie looked ahead.

"It looks as if the road starts going downhill past that bend. But there aren't any trees on that side of the road."

"It must have been here somewhere." Gran was determined. "Maybe there's another bend further on. I'm going to walk a little further on."

"I'll bring the car, Gran."

"No, it can't be far away. I'll just walk to that old tree stump . . . oh!"

Gran stopped in her tracks, suddenly realising what she was looking at.

"This was it. The Corncochle Tree. You were right enough, Chrissie. It's been cut down."

Her voice was smaller now as she began to walk once more, stepping slowly, almost reverently, towards the stump of her precious old tree.

Chrissie followed, struggling to swallow a lump in her throat.

She was surprised at the depth of her disappointment. How could she feel so bad at the loss of an old tree that she'd never heard of until yesterday?

If she could feel this badly about it, she couldn't begin to imagine how Gran must be feeling.

"Actually, it doesn't look as if it was cut," Gran said as she reached the fence. "It would have been much neater if it had. These branches wouldn't have been left all straggly like this. It looks as if it snapped."

"Maybe the branches cracked in a high wind," Chrissie suggested. "It's quite exposed up here."

"It could have been struck by lightning!" Gran said, ever dramatic. She gave an impish grin. "Well, I'm glad I'm not going doolally, after all. It was the right road.

"Look, the hill goes down from here. I can remember the feeling of freedom, of adventure – it really took my breath away."

She looked down the hill, remembering.

"I'm so glad we found it again, even though . . ."

"Gran! Gran, look!" Chrissie pointed to the tree stump, eyes shining.

Gran looked more closely and a rush of joy flowed through her. Nestled in the gnarled and wizened cracks of the old tree stump were dozens of tiny new pale green shoots, sprouting from where the branches had snapped off.

"Oh, you dear old tree," she breathed.

Chrissie took several photographs as Gran stood, lost in thought. This was one moment which they definitely had to capture before they left for home.

It was quite some time before they were able to drag themselves away.

"You know," Gran remarked, as they walked back to the car, "it's not giving up, is it? It's taken a knock, but it's starting again. Life goes on."

Gran took one last look back as they fastened their seatbelts. Chrissie started the engine and pulled out on to the road once more.

As the car gathered speed, Nellie closed her eyes and imagined she was on her bike once more, freewheeling down the hill, leaving the Corncochle Tree far behind. ■

Market Day

by Natalie Kleinman

I WAS wrapping Dad's sandwiches in some greaseproof paper when he walked into the kitchen.

"You can make one for yourself and come with me, if you like," he suggested. "Your mother's going over to Auntie May's later and I know her cat makes you sneeze. Bring a book in case you get bored."

"Can I, Daddy? Really?"

"Didn't I just say so? Get on with you, then, Judy. You've got ten minutes."

The next cheese sandwich wasn't the most elegant I'd ever made, but I knew Dad was in a hurry. I was careful to wipe the yellow Formica-topped table, though. It was Mum's pride and joy, and she did like her kitchen kept tidy.

I didn't think for one moment that I'd need a book, but I took it anyway.

Dad was already sitting in the car when I got outside, looking at his watch as if impatient to go, but I knew he was teasing. He teased me a lot, but I didn't mind.

I slid into the front seat next to him, a real treat for me. That place was usually reserved for Mum.

"Right," he said, looking into his rear-view mirror, signalling and pulling gently out into our suburban London road. "We're off."

I'd not long turned eleven and I was on top of the world and feeling not a little proud.

In these post-war days of the mid-Fifties there was still euphoria in the country, a sense of hope and a determination to do one's best in a world that was safe once more.

Not everybody had a car, but my dad worked in a garage and he'd got it cheap. Apart from this weekly journey and the occasional Saturday family outing into the countryside, Sally remained parked outside our terraced house.

Mum had said, at the start of one of those early outings, "Let's sally forth, then," and the car had been called Sally ever since.

* * * *

The market, which took close to an hour to get to, was in the city on a long, straight road that was lined with shops on both sides.

In front of the shops, leaving room for people to walk between them, was a row of stalls, some looking rather skeletal as we arrived.

After parking the car, we stopped outside a general store and my father told me to wait while he went inside.

I looked at the stall, its wooden frame not appearing sturdy enough for the load it was about to hold, but when I grabbed one of the uprights it felt firm enough.

There was an awning on top in case it rained, but at that moment it was rolled back and a glorious early morning summer sun shone down on what seemed to me like a fairy-tale land.

"Don't stand there gawping, girl. You may as well give me a hand while you're here," Dad moaned, his arms holding what was obviously a weighty box. "Get out back and see if you can bring some of that stuff out with you."

He set the box on the stall.

Illustration by iStock.

"Nothing too heavy, mind. We don't want you dropping it and breaking something."

I was delighted to be able to help, and didn't Dad know it!

He was a kindly, hard-working man and he'd taught me and my younger sister Peggy that if something was worth having it was worth making sacrifices for.

The whole family sacrificed their Sundays, but we didn't mind because Dad told us he was determined to earn enough to give us all a few little luxuries now and then.

The war wasn't so distant that we'd forgotten what it was like to go without, even me, what with rationing only ending the year before.

Dad had told me that he paid a fee to the proprietor of the shop behind his stall to store his goods out back.

"I made several trips to Stoke-on-Trent when I started doing the market. Where the potteries are, if you haven't done that in school yet. Poor Sally, carrying all that china!

"I was fearful for her suspension, but Joe, my boss at the garage, offered to lend me his van. 'Just so long as you pay for the petrol, it's no skin off my nose,' he said, and luckily after that Sally didn't have to take the strain."

"Why china, Dad?" I asked him, fascinated at the way he was dressing his stall.

"It was your mum, really. Most of our stuff was chipped and we couldn't afford an expensive new set. She was that upset when the teapot broke.

"Then a friend asked me to help him out one weekend when his wife's mum couldn't look after their kiddies. I don't suppose I would ever have thought of it on my own, but I love it. And it lets me buy your mother and you one or two extras that we would otherwise be unable to afford."

As I looked around I could see that most of the other stalls were either "dressed" or nearly so.

The street between our stall and those on the other side was nearly empty, but the first trickle of customers and onlookers had begun to filter in.

It was barely nine o'clock and Dad told me that before long people would be brushing shoulder to shoulder to get past each other.

"If you want to explore, do it now, before it gets too busy," he advised me.

I didn't need telling twice!

The noise and bustle were already building as I moved to the next stall. It was laid out with every kind of sweet imaginable, and even some the like of which I'd never seen before.

In glorious colour there were liquorice all-sorts, toffees, sherbet lemons, chocolate buttons covered with hundreds and thousands, marshmallows, cough sweets, barley sugar and flying saucers.

I can still feel my mouth watering all these years later.

"They're a ha'penny each," Doris said, seeing me eyeing the saucers, "but you can have three for a penny-farthing."

I pulled the pockets of my blazer inside-out to demonstrate their empty state and smiled regretfully, but the woman on the stall was a kindly soul, and in any case, she knew my dad.

"Here y'are, love. Seein' as 'ow we're sort of neighbours, you can pick one if you like, just this once."

Mindful of my manners, with a big thank you I moved happily on, the rice paper sticking to my lips as I sucked at the sherbet inside.

Next I came to a haberdashery stall, almost as colourful as the one I'd just left. Needles and cottons, buttons and ribbons.

Mum had a box at home full of buttons. Round ones, square ones, glass ones and my favourites, those that resembled pearls.

"My dad said he'll give me tuppence for helping him out today. Would you mind putting this pearl button aside for me and I'll come back and pay for it later?" I asked shyly but feeling very grown up.

The lady behind the stall held out her hand and I leaned forward and dropped the button into her palm.

"I'll put it in this 'ere box. Don't you forget now."

"I won't, I promise."

✳　✳　✳　✳

I spent an hour or so wandering up and down, fascinated by the variety of goods and stallholders.

Some sat on stools waiting to be approached; others shouted out their wares with good-natured humour.

There was one called Gerry.

"Gerry's the name, clothes is my game," he cried.

And did he sell clothes! Really sell them.

He stood on a box behind the display holding a pile of jumpers in assorted colours in one hand. Then he put them down and picked them up, just one at a time, creating the pile all over again, talking all the while.

"How much do I want for these lovely jumpers? Here are two best-quality jumpers. You won't see better this side of the West End. Or cheaper. Do I want three nicker? Do I want two nicker? One nicker? Nah."

Each time he mentioned a price he'd bang his hand down.

"Ten bob! Who'll give me ten bob for two jumpers? There you are, darlin'. Sold to the lady in the red coat."

"How about you, sweetheart? I've got a lovely blue dress here to match your eyes," he said, turning his attention to another.

So quick was his patter, the public could hardly keep up with him, and they couldn't give him their money fast enough.

I wasn't a bit surprised when the blue-eyed lady held the dress up against her before saying eagerly that she'd take it.

✳　✳　✳　✳

By the time I got back to where Dad had just finished serving a customer, I was starving.

Making my way through hadn't been all that easy, especially when a small crowd had gathered in front of a stall selling all kinds of cloth.

There were bales, large folded remnants and small scraps. Cards of lace. It was a kaleidoscope of hues and shapes and patterns.

The purveyor of these wonderful goods was a large woman who shouted out her wares in just such a booming voice as Gerry had, and to just as good effect.

Next to her, a man, whom I presumed to be her husband, was measuring and cutting off the required lengths, which he folded neatly and placed into a paper bag.

My mum made all my clothes. And hers and my sister's, so I wasn't surprised this stall was so busy.

"It's amazing," I told Dad when finally I reached him. "I'm glad you brought me. Is it lunchtime yet?"

"Are you hungry already? It's barely eleven o'clock. Go on, then, we did get off to a very early start," he said as I tried to adopt the demeanour of a poor starving orphan.

I sat down on a small stool next to him, chewing thoughtfully as he served his customers.

In his own way he was just as good a salesman as Gerry. Just not as loud.

"Are you finished? Here's that tuppence I promised you, then," Dad said. "Before you go running off again, though, could you get me a cup of tea from the stall over there? And some lemonade for you, if you like."

Stallholders began packing away at about three o'clock, but it still felt like it had been a long day, what with the early start and being on my feet most of the day which I wasn't used to.

I'd been back for the pearl button, which was now safely tucked away in my breast pocket, and what was left over had gone on two more flying saucers.

There were some gaps on Dad's stall, so hopefully he'd had a good day, but it was still hard work helping him carry what was left into the back of the shop.

It had been a really hot day and the sun was still shining as we drove home.

Its warmth and the motion of the car sent me off to sleep.

I was embarrassed when I woke up because at eleven I was far too old and dignified to need an afternoon nap.

It was OK, though, because Dad pretended he hadn't noticed.

I raced into the house, where my mum and my sister were in the kitchen, not long home themselves.

"Auntie May sends her love. Did you have a good time?" Mum asked me.

"I'd like to go again if Dad will take me. Here, I got you something," I declared, taking the button from my top pocket. "To add to your collection."

"That's really pretty. Thank you, darling."

"I got you something, too," I continued, turning to Peggy.

I handed her one of the two flying saucers.

"But be careful. I sucked on mine and started coughing because the sherbet went down my throat the wrong way.

"It wasn't as bad as if I'd gone to Auntie May and started sneezing, though."

Dad walked into the kitchen waving something in his hand.

"You left this in the car, Judy," he said, handing it to me before kissing my mother and sister on the cheek.

It was my book, the one he'd suggested I take to read in case I was bored.

I'd forgotten all about it. ∎

EVERYDAY VALUE

Flour

Decorations

Meat

Vegetables

Desserts

On The Shelf

I'M really rather puzzled,
Why every time I shop
I realise I'm months behind.
It makes me stand and stop.

It's "Back to School" pre-summer,
Then on to Hallowe'en,
At turbo pace it's fireworks,
No lingering between.

Christmas starts September,
The music plays too long,
The holiday ads next in line,
Before the tinsel's gone.

There's hot cross buns in February,
Then Easter eggs in rows,
The holiday shop range never stops,
And on and on it goes!

So let's reject the pressure,
To buy before the date.
I'm steering clear of seasonal aisles –
The shops will have to wait!

Judy Jarvie

iStock.

Cheery And Bubbly

by Donald Lightwood

THE pub's lounge was large and attractively furnished. Martin looked around at the tables until he spotted a woman by herself.

"Excuse me, are you Bubbly, by any chance?"

She looked at him with a mixture of surprise and relief.

"Yes, and you must be Cheery?"

He nodded and sat down at her table. They smiled, each doing a quick assessment of the other.

"I haven't been here before," he told her.

"Me, neither."

They fell silent and glanced around the room.

"So, we both wrote to Meet A Mate," he ventured.

"I wondered if it would work, to tell the truth," she said. "Asking for a one-word description of yourself seemed ridiculous."

"I suppose it's meant to be a sort of guide to your character."

"And I mean, you don't want to put people off," she went on.

He nodded and wondered what to say.

"What did you expect from my name, Cheery?" he asked.

"Well, a happy person, full of smiles, I suppose."

He frowned.

"I hoped it would attract somebody. It seems to have worked."

"It did. But if you don't mind me saying so, you don't seem all that cheery. Though I'm not particularly bubbly, either."

There was silence.

"My real name's Audrey," she said.

"Martin."

They exchanged a small smile.

"I'd love to be bubbly," she confided.

He nodded.

"I'd like to be cheery."

"The thing is, how do you do it?"

The lounge was full of couples. Giggles and laughter punctuated the murmur of conversation.

"Look at those two," Audrey said, nodding at a couple by the bar, absorbed in laughter. "He's all smiles and she's full of giggles. I've grown up being envious of people like that."

Martin knew how she felt. Naturally reserved, he always seemed to be on the outside.

The couple said something to each other and the man approached Martin and Audrey's table.

"Excuse me. Do you know us?" he asked.

The two realised they'd been staring.

"We . . ." Martin began.

"We noticed how happy you were,"

Illustration by Mandy Dixon.

Audrey explained. "You seem to be having a good time."

Surprised, the man gave a broad smile.

"I didn't expect that!" He looked around. It was getting busier by the minute. "We've been hoping to grab a seat but they're all taken."

He glanced at the two empty seats at their table.

"Unless – do you mind if we join you?"

Martin and Audrey exchanged a quick look.

"Well, yes, OK," Audrey said, and the man called his girlfriend over.

"Thanks. My feet were killing me – new shoes," she said with a grimace as she sank gratefully on to the chair.

They fell quite naturally into chatting, all four of them. The couple were just a few years younger than Audrey and Martin, and worked at the local hospital. Rita was a nurse and Jim a paramedic.

"It must be difficult getting time off together," Audrey said.

The two nodded.

"It is, especially for Jim," Rita agreed.

"A demanding job," Martin commented and Jim nodded.

"You never know what's coming up. Road accidents are the worst."

"It's depressing, so we don't talk about it," Rita told them. "We decided to be cheerful instead."

"You just decided?" Audrey said, and they nodded.

Martin shook his head.

"Well, it seems to have worked." He paused. "Actually, this is the first time we've met," he explained. "Neither of us is what we expected."

"Which is why we were staring at you, wondering how you did it," Audrey added.

Jim smiled.

"It's what we do every day, isn't it? Pretend to be something we're not, whether it's confident, brave or funny. It's a game, and eventually you find you're playing it all the time."

There was a silence. Martin and Audrey looked at them, and then at each other.

"At least give it a try."

"Maybe we will," Audrey said, and they moved on to chat about other things.

* * * *

Martin walked Audrey home.

"What do you think?" he asked at her gate.

"What have we got to lose?"

"OK. I'll give you a call."

They saw each other next on a Sunday afternoon and went to the park. They'd both been thinking about Jim and Rita's advice.

Consciously or not, Audrey had copied Rita's colourful top and Martin had opted for a T-shirt and jeans, like Jim.

They were both surprised by each other.

"Hello," Martin said.

"Hello. You look different."

"You, too." They exchanged a smile.

The park was busy with people enjoying the sun. They joined them, wondering what to say.

"What Jim and Rita said was interesting, wasn't it?" she asked. "About pretending to be what you want to be."

"It was. I've been thinking about it a lot," he admitted.

"Me, too." She nodded. "So, how do we start?"

"I think we already have," he said, indicating their change of clothes.

"Oh, look!" she cried, pointing up. "Somebody's kite has got away. I loved the kite scenes in 'Mary Poppins'."

"I remember it made me want to be a chimney sweep."

At that moment a football came bouncing towards them. Martin trapped it with his foot and flicked the ball up before kicking it back.

"That was clever," Audrey commented.

"When I didn't become a sweep, I planned to be an international footballer instead. But that didn't work out, either."

They watched the busy trade around an ice-cream van.

"Like one?" he said.

"No, thank you, I shouldn't."

"Why not?"

She shrugged.

"Oh, you know, watching my weight and all that stuff."

"I know what you mean," he agreed. "But one wouldn't hurt, would it?"

"Then thank you, I'll have a cone. Vanilla."

They sat on a bench to eat them.

"That was delicious," she said. "And I don't feel a bit guilty."

"I promise not to tell," he said.

She laughed and they rose to wander towards the playground.

"I used to love the swings," she said.

One of the swings was free and Audrey gazed at it.

"I'd love a shot."

"Go on, I dare you."

She looked around then dashed to the swing and sat down on it.

"Hold on, I'll give you a push."

Within moments she was going back and forward, higher and higher.

"What do you think you're doing?" a man's voice shouted.

The park keeper!

Audrey slowed the swing down.

"I couldn't help it," she told him.

"Even so, the swings are meant for the kids," the man said. "Now, go away and don't come back."

*   *   *   *

"Did you see his face?" Audrey was giggling as they skulked away. Martin laughed.

"I've a good mind to go and have a shot on the slide."

"Oh, no, please!" she cried. "Let's have another ice-cream instead."

They settled on their bench again, enjoying strawberry cones this time.

"You did it, though," he said.

"I can't believe it." She shook her head. "It must be you. You're either good for me or bad. I can't make up my mind which."

"When do you think you'll know?"

"When I stop enjoying myself."

"Maybe you won't."

"I'm bound to. I have to go home, cook the tea, clean my teeth, go to bed."

He laughed.

"We all have to do that stuff."

"Seriously, what they said about pretending?" she went on. "I haven't been. I mean, things just happened. What about you?"

"I forgot all about it," he said. "Being with you seemed to do the trick."

It occurred to Audrey that that was the nicest thing she'd ever heard.

"Are your fingers sticky?" she asked.

He nodded.

"Good, so are mine," she said, taking hold of his hand.

They sighed and their bench suddenly seemed incredibly comfortable.

They might not be cheery and bubbly, but they seemed to suit each other. It was a pleasant feeling.

Jim and Rita had helped them. They had persuaded them to try.

"Monday tomorrow," she said. "I feel fine about going back to work."

He grinned.

"So do I."

"It must mean that we're happy."

His face lit up and he carefully unstuck his hand from hers and put his arm round her shoulder.

"Cheery," she said.

"Bubbly," he replied. ▪

Magical Olympic Moments

1992

When Essex girl Sally Gunnell headed to Barcelona to compete in the 400m hurdles there were high hopes of a medal. After all, the British former track and field athlete had come so close to gold just a year before at Tokyo's 1991 World Championships. A moment's glance at a rival had been enough to break Gunnell's rhythm and she'd had to settle for silver.

This time, though, she had her sights firmly set on gold. In the end she won comfortably and stepped up to the podium and into the history books. When she crossed the line her hands flew to her face, as if Gunnell couldn't quite believe she'd done it. Her lap of honour let her soak up the atmosphere and the realisation that she had, indeed, captured her golden moment.

Sally managed to win bronze as part of the 4x400m relay team, too, making it a very successful Games. Overall, her sporting career was so successful that she held Commonwealth, European, World and Olympic track titles simultaneously. ■

A Fairy Godmother

Illustration by Philip Crabb.

by Alyson Hilbourne

MUM! Is there anything I can take for lunch? We're out on a field trip all day."

Sarah stepped into the kitchen to find Caitlin yanking open cupboards and peering inside.

"Why didn't you tell me last night?"

"I forgot."

Sarah sighed and pulled herself up straight.

"Right." She moved over to the fridge. "Here's an apple."

She got out the cheese and cut off a chunk.

"Wrap this in cling film, and there are some oatcakes somewhere."

She reached up to the cupboard and moved things about, searching. She found a few bourbon biscuits, and filled a water flask.

Caitlin shoved everything in her bag and blew Sarah a kiss.

"Thanks, Mum! See you this evening."

"Have a good day," Sarah called, but Caitlin was already out of sight.

She'd barely turned round when a voice wafted down the stairs.

"Sarah? Have you seen my blue tie? I can't find it anywhere."

Sarah walked back through the kitchen to the hall.

"I haven't moved it," she called back. "It should be in the wardrobe."

"Well, it's not here." Her husband's voice was plaintive.

A twitch of annoyance crossed Sarah's face, and she trudged upstairs. Dave was in the bedroom, pulling drawers open.

"Dave, stop! Why would it be in with my sweaters?"

"Well, it's not in the wardrobe."

"Let me look." Sarah pulled out the tie rack. It wasn't there. She looked on the floor of the cupboard, moving shoes and boots.

"Aha!" She pounced. "Here it is. It was in your walking boot."

Dave came over, took the tie and planted a kiss on Sarah's cheek.

"Thanks, love."

Out in the hall again, Sarah almost collided with her son, Jason.

"Mum? Have you seen my football kit?"

Sarah frowned.

"Did you put it in the wash when you last wore it?"

Jason shrugged, avoiding Sarah's eye.

Sarah went into his room and bent down to look under the bed. It wasn't there. She stood up and looked behind the door, Jason's usual dumping ground.

She picked up a fleece that shouldn't have been there.

"Is this it?" She held up a bag.

"Oh, yes! Thanks, Mum."

"It's not washed."

"Doesn't matter. Gotta dash. Before-school training . . ."

Ten minutes later, the house was quiet and Sarah sat down at the kitchen table with a mug of tea.

Some days she felt like Cinderella tidying up after the family. Oh, she loved them to bits, but she wished they'd take some responsibility for their own things. Every morning was the same.

She looked around at the hurricane-swept house. What she needed was a fairy godmother; someone to wave a wand and take her away from all this.

But fairy godmothers didn't exist in suburban England.

She shook her head. She'd go out shopping before dealing with the mess here. It would make her feel better.

* * * *

"Bread, milk, veggies, cereal, cheese." Sarah repeated the shopping list in her head like a mantra. "Burgers for dinner, perhaps."

She was pushing a trolley along the cereal aisle when something hit her thigh. She looked down into the face of a toddler in the baby seat of another trolley. There was a bag of crisps at her feet.

When she bent to pick them up, she noticed a trail of items all along the aisle.

"Oh," she said, smiling at the toddler. "Are you having fun? What's Mummy going to cook for dinner if you throw everything out?"

The mother of the child turned round then and noticed the missing items.

"Oh, Harry. Not again. Thank you so much." She took the crisps from Sarah. "He does love doing this. Shopping is a nightmare."

Sarah smiled.

"No worries," she said. "Let me get them for you, and maybe you can stack them further away." She collected the bits and pieces up, and gave them to the fraught mother. Then she waved goodbye to the toddler.

"Excuse me, miss? Can you help?"

Sarah turned, unsure if the voice was directed at her. A lady was waving a walking stick in her direction.

Sarah blinked. She wasn't in uniform. Did this woman think she worked in the store?

"I can't get the tins from the top shelf. It's too high."

"Let me." Sarah reached up. "This one?"

"Yes, please. Two, please."

Sarah handed the woman the tins, and she bobbed a thank you and wobbled off down the aisle.

Sarah smiled after her. Even in the supermarket, she couldn't escape finding things for other people.

* * * *

As she pulled into the drive, Sarah's eyes widened. Her pregnant neighbour, Annalisa, was standing awkwardly, gripping the joining fence.

"Are you OK, Annalisa?" Sarah asked, concerned.

"My contractions have started, and I can't get hold of John. I don't know what to do with Mollie." Annalisa's voice was choked.

"Have you got your bag ready? I'll take Mollie, but let's get you to hospital first. It'll be quicker if I drive."

She followed Annalisa to the house and helped bundle three-year-old Mollie into a jacket and shoes. Then she supported Annalisa under the arm, and helped her into the passenger seat of her car.

"It's a tight fit." Sarah laughed.

She popped Mollie in the back and buckled the seat belt, grimacing about the lack of a car seat.

"Sit still, Mollie," she said. "We've got to take Mummy to the hospital." The little girl sucked her thumb and looked back at her solemnly.

Sarah drove slowly and carefully. Her jaw clenched every time Annalisa gave a moan of pain, and Mollie a whimper of fear.

At the hospital entrance, she dashed inside to find a porter. As Annalisa was helped into a wheelchair, Sarah got back in the car.

"I'll find a parking spot and we'll come inside," she called out.

"Mummmmmy!" Mollie sobbed, stretching her hands out.

"It's OK, sweetie. We'll park the car, then we'll go and see Mummy."

She steered the car into the car park and finally found a space. Then she and Mollie walked back to the hospital building.

Upstairs in the maternity unit, a particularly officious nurse wouldn't let them in to see Annalisa.

"Are you family? Only family or nominated birthing partners allowed." Sarah shook her head.

"We'll wait," she said. "Her husband should be here soon."

She and Mollie sat on the plastic chairs, watching the doctors and nurses to-ing and fro-ing. "People watching" calmed the child down, and by the time John arrived, Mollie was chuckling away with Sarah.

"Thank you, thank you!" He gasped. "I was in a meeting. Couldn't get away."

"Don't worry. I'll take Mollie home with me."

"Be a good girl for Sarah," John said to his daughter, dropping a kiss on her head. "Daddy will come and get you as soon as I can."

* * * *

That afternoon Sarah raided Caitlin and Jason's rooms for coloured pencils and paper, and found some of their old storybooks that Mollie could look at.

Mollie liked the fairy stories. After Sarah made a sandwich for lunch, they settled on the sofa with a book about fairies and witches.

Mollie wanted "Cinderella", and then "Snow White" with the good fairy. Sarah was still reading, though Mollie was asleep, when Jason came in.

"Whatcha doing, Mum?" he asked.

"Reading Mollie a story."

"She's asleep."

"Yes, but as soon as I move she'll wake up. Could you get the shopping in from the car? I haven't had a chance. My keys are on the side."

Caitlin came home next.

"Ah, sweet," she said. "She's asleep."

Sarah tried to put Mollie down, but she whimpered as Sarah edged her off her lap. In the end, Dave cooked dinner for the family.

"This is lovely," Sarah said. "A real treat."

It was late when John finally called to collect Mollie.

"A lovely boy," he said, a smile splitting his face. "Sorry to have been so long. After the initial panic, it all took longer than expected."

"Have you had a good time, Ms Mollie?" he asked.

"Yes, I saw a fairy godmother," Mollie told her father.

"That's great. Well, tomorrow you can see your baby brother, and we'll go and get Mummy from hospital."

"If you need any help, just shout," Sarah said.

But it was a few days before she saw her neighbours again. When the doorbell sounded, she opened it to find Annalisa holding the baby, and John holding Mollie's hand. In her other hand Mollie held an envelope.

"Hello. Come in, won't you? Oh, look at him! Isn't he tiny?"

They went into the living-room and Mollie thrust the envelope at her.

"It's for you," Mollie said. "For being a fairy."

Sarah's eyebrows shot up.

"Sorry," Annalisa said. "It's a thank-you for looking after Mollie and taking me to hospital. I don't know what I'd have done without you. Mollie loved the fairies in those stories you read her." She smiled.

"And Mummy, ask her!" Mollie danced from foot to foot.

"Ah, John and I would like to ask you to be a godmother –"

"No, a fairy godmother," Mollie said, her hands clenched.

"A fairy godmother," Annalisa corrected herself. "To Paul. Actually Mollie would like you to be her godmother, but she already has one."

Sarah felt her face colouring.

"I'd be delighted. Now, what's in here?" She looked at the envelope.

"A thank-you," Annalisa said. "From John's company."

Sarah opened the envelope. Inside was a voucher for a spa day at the Lakes Hotel.

"Oh, how thoughtful of you," Sarah said. "There was really no need."

"You helped us out," John said. "I'm not sure what would have happened if you hadn't been around."

"Well, thanks. I will enjoy that," Sarah said.

Some dedicated time to herself, she thought. How wonderful.

Her fairy godmother must have been listening, after all. ■

Horsey Windpump, Norfolk

THERE has been a drainage mill in the village of Horsey on the Norfolk Broads since the 18th century. The pumps are needed to transfer water from the dykes that drain the low-lying land to the higher level system of tidal waterways that reach the sea at Great Yarmouth, 23 miles away.

   Lying next to Horsey Mere, the wind-powered pump was built in 1912 on the foundations of an older structure. Like many windpumps in the area, Horsey Mill was converted to diesel power in the early twentieth century. A Grade-II-listed building owned by the National Trust, the mill is open to the public. As well as exploring the mill, visitors can explore the wildlife site on the Horsey estate, to see marsh harriers, swallowtail butterflies, bitterns and kingfishers. ■

Ruby's Garden

by Sylvie Hall

H E heard Ruby before he saw her.

"I won't be long, Mummy! I'm saying bye to my friend!"

It was bellowed down the length of next door's garden.

What a strong pair of lungs for such a little body, he thought, not for the first time.

Keeping his head down, he waited as she ran down the garden, stood on her tiptoes and shouted over the garden fence.

"Hiya, Stan!"

He placed his hand on his chest, exaggerating a startled response.

"Oh, Ruby! What a fright you gave me."

It made her giggle, as it was meant to.

Her face was just visible.

"What are you doing, Stan?"

"I'm just putting baby onions and shallots in the ground," he said.

With much theatrical groaning, he rose from his kneeling stool.

Ruby laughed.

"Babies? You are so funny, Stan."

"Yes, and if I look after them properly, they'll grow up and we can eat them all up," he said with relish, which made her giggle again.

She executed an elegant twirl, to better give the effect of her outfit.

"Me and Mummy are going to Holly's house for a play-date," she announced. "I have my princess dress on."

"Yes, I can see that, and very pretty it is, too."

Ruby gave a satisfied nod, then lifted her skirts and sprinted up to her mum, Fiona, who was waiting at their conservatory door.

"See you later, Stan!" she shouted.

Gemma had counselled restraint when sowing and planting out his vegetables, and every year, Stan produced more than they could use. But he liked gifting spare tomatoes, courgettes or whatever to family and friends. Nevertheless, as he laid out the beds this year, he was aware that the whole operation needed to be cut back even more.

Illustration by Mandy Dixon.

Stan coped best when he was occupied, and after what had been a difficult winter, he took solace in the hard toil of growing things.

Taking a break to observe some cows in the adjoining field, he cast his mind back to when this and the neighbouring gardens had been hives of children, buzzing back and forth through gates and over fences to play their noisy games.

His own children were middle-aged now, and his grandchildren young adults. No more rowdy Sunday dinners with family spilling into the garden. He was now the guest in their homes.

Stan sighed, and reminded himself that his daughters, their husbands and the grandchildren had been a great support and comfort during these past months. Neighbours, too, had been very kind.

He remembered the day, nearly five years ago, when Darren and Fiona had broken the news that they were expecting a baby, to add to their three teenage boys.

It seemed like only yesterday he'd watched Gemma's face light up when Fiona handed two-day-old Ruby across the garden fence. They took turns holding her, and he remembered Gemma's eyes welling up with emotion in memory of the babies that had gone before.

There's nothing like a new baby to bring out tender and protective feelings in a person, he thought, both then and now.

Darren and Fiona dubbed Ruby their "bonus child". Gemma had often commented that she was their little bonus child, too. They were very fond of her, as she was of them.

Among her first clutch of words, "Stan" and "Gemma" were often heard clearly, as she reached her arms out to be passed over the fence.

She'd demanded to be let through the gate that connected the gardens as soon as she could walk, so that she could walk on the soft grass and inspect the flower-beds. Occasionally, she ventured into Stan's vegetable plot, but mostly it was the flowers that held her attention.

As he got back to preparing soil and assembling frameworks, Stan thought about the extra zest little Ruby had brought to their lives, and remembered two generations of children working here alongside him.

As he worked, the seed of an idea was sown and began to germinate in his mind.

∗   ∗   ∗   ∗

Two days later, he was ready to put his proposal to Fiona.

"Morning. Where's the little one? At nursery school, is she?"

"Yes. We can both get a bit of peace and quiet. I worry that she's a bit of a nuisance to you, Stan."

"Not a bit of it. She's a breath of fresh air," he reassured her. "I wondered — what do you think to the idea of her having a little bit of my veggie plot, for some easy-to-grow vegetables?"

"That's kind of you, Stan, but are you sure it's not too much for you?"

"Not at all. She's no bother."

"Thanks, Stan, she'd love it. Let's face it, she'll not get the chance with Darren and me. Neither of us has green fingers."

He cast his eyes over the football nets, swings and trampoline behind Fiona.

"Yours is a playing garden, not a growing garden. Nothing wrong with that."

∗   ∗   ∗   ∗

"Have you decided what veggie-tables to grow in Ruby's garden?" Stan asked a very excited Ruby later that day.

Her veggie-table of choice — carrots — did not fill Stan with confidence.

"They're a bit tricky, carrots, what with the threat of carrot fly and wonky roots," he explained to Ruby, who listened with the intensity of an eager four-and-a-half-year-old.

"I think we need to sow a couple of rows of scallions among these carrots," he advised.

"Scallions?" Ruby giggled at the word. "What are scallions?"

"Spring onions. It's the smell, you see. Carrot flies like the smell of carrots, and bite holes in them, but hate the smell of anything oniony."

Attentively, Ruby nodded her understanding.

Together they prepared and sowed a corner of Stan's vegetable patch, which was marked with a sign proclaiming to the world that this little square of earth was *Ruby's Garden*.

Ruby's devotion to her "patch" over the summer was somewhat hit and miss, and subject to a busy diary of half-days at nursery school, play-dates and summer holidays with her parents and older siblings.

Conversely, Stan's social calendar – consisting of trips to the shops, leek club, dominoes club and monthly history group – left plenty of time to tend the areas of potatoes, roots, brassicas, legumes and sweetcorn.

In spite of scaling down the whole set-up this year, Stan's family, friends and neighbours benefited from the fruits of his labour. It didn't matter to him; he loved nothing better than the feel of his hands in the soil in "the working end" of the garden.

During the summer, activities notwithstanding, there were plenty of opportunities for Ruby to present herself in her "garden clothes" and pink wellies, to be let through the gate to work alongside Stan.

It brought a smile to Stan's face to watch her inspect the progress of the plants. She walked up and down the rows of broad beans and peas, held to attention by bamboo canes and peasticks, and stared intently at neat rows of radishes, plump lettuces, and the sprawl of courgettes.

But mostly she loved to gossip about her friends.

"Holly won't eat vegetables," she said one day. "She only eats peas. She won't grow up strong, will she?"

"I don't play with Oscar now," she told him in the middle of another gardening excursion. "He doesn't know how to share."

Stan's main role in these conversations was to make encouraging noises, or to ask clarifying questions, but he tried to supplement his responses with a little education. He drew her attention to bees pollinating the plants; told her about the importance of worms in the garden; gave gentle guidance in performing manageable tasks.

Fiona kept the garden watered and the tomatoes happy during Stan's trips to visit relatives or old pals. When he returned, Ruby regaled him with in-depth reports about the care of his beloved patch, and an account of the "veggie-tables" the family had picked during his absence.

Against the odds, the small, round carrots – chosen specifically for their prettiness – thrived, and were harvested. Ruby was delighted.

An image of the proud gardeners, a container of their produce between them, was posted on a social media site by Fiona. Stan didn't know much about that himself, but he was secretly chuffed.

Late on a hot afternoon at the tail end of August, with tasks completed in the working end of the garden, Stan's attention was drawn to what Gemma had once christened "the pretty quarter".

The apple tree, heavy with fruit, made him realise that autumn was around the corner, and that it was nearly a year since Gemma had passed away. She had always kept the top end as pretty as a picture.

"This garden needs colour," he said to himself. "It needs flowers. I reckon I could manage a few flowers next year."

He made his way over to the fence and saw Darren and Ruby playing in their garden.

"How's it going?" his neighbour asked.

Stan pretended not to see Ruby, who was tugging her father's shorts.

"Not bad," he said. "Mind you, these shrubs are in need of a session of rehydration. Do you know anybody that can help me with that?"

Jumping up and down, Ruby held her hand aloft.

"Oh, Ruby! I didn't see you there. I could do with some of your expertise with the hose in this thirsty garden."

Ruby's favourite job in the garden was watering anything that might benefit from a drenching, including herself. She liked to be in charge of the spray gun, which, with glee, she changed through the settings from shower to jet.

Stan and Darren watched as, with squeals of delight, Ruby created what she called "baby rainbows'" with her spraying.

"I think that'll do for now," Stan said after a while. "A brilliant job, Ruby. You deserve some apple juice."

"Can I have a biscuit with it, please?" Ruby asked.

"Seeing as you've asked nicely, why don't we have two?"

As Stan and Ruby settled into their chairs on the decking, she opened the conversation.

"Did you know my mummy is clever? She can read upside down."

"That is clever. It's like a superpower. Can you read upside down?"

"I can't even read properly yet! But I can write my own name."

"Clever girl! It's a good job you're starting school next week. I reckon you're ready for all that reading and writing."

Ruby broke the short companionable silence which followed.

"Gemma was my oldest best friend."

"Yes, she was my oldest best friend, too."

"Now Gemma isn't here any more, you are my very oldest best friend."

"I'm glad. And you know what? You're my youngest best friend."

"Gemma and me used to eat flowers," Ruby said, as she cast her eye over the sparse borders.

"You did. Gemma was a one for her flowers. We've got plenty of the ones I know you can eat. Nasturtiums, they're called. They're down the side of the house, up the fence, and growing up the back of the shed. Gemma left no shortage of nasturtiums in this garden."

"Nasty-mums? Stan, you are funny!"

"Nasty-mums? Yes, that's near enough."

It was late afternoon. Stan and Ruby basked in the glory of their friendship – which straddled not only the garden fence, but also the age divide – as they walked the garden in search of their favourite colours of "nasty-mums", from the palest of yellows through orange to the darkest of reds.

Careful to shake and blow the flower heads free of any lurking little bugs, Stan and Ruby ate the flowers in remembrance of Gemma.

"Stan, next year can we grow broccoli? It's my new favourite," Ruby said, as they walked to the gate where Darren was calling her in for tea.

"Good choice. Broccoli it is, then. And some flowers. We'll grow some flowers, too." ■

Magical Olympic Moments

2000

Steve Redgrave rode the crest of the wave for five consecutive Olympic Games, winning gold each time from 1984 to the Sydney Olympics in 2000. His Los Angeles win in 1984 was to be the first of his handful of golds, followed by Seoul in 1988, Barcelona in 1992, Atlanta in 1996 and Sydney in 2000 – his consecutive run an unrivalled record which stands to this day.

With a catalogue of golden wins in World Championships and Commonwealth Games over the years, too, he is undoubtedly the greatest rower of all time. His wins are all the more impressive when you consider he had to battle through illnesses including type-2 diabetes. That final gold in Sydney was right down to the wire, with the coxless four of Redgrave, along with Matthew Pinsent, James Cracknell and Tim Foster, winning by 0.38 of a second as they beat tough rivals Italy into second place, followed by Australia.

Dominating in the water, the men's eight also attained gold, as did Ben Ainslie, Shirley Robertson and Iain Percy in their respective sailing events. The 2000 Olympics proved Great Britain's most successful Summer Olympics since 1920 with 11 gold, 10 silver and seven bronze medals. ■

Meet Me At The Bridge

by Christine Bryant

T
HIS is ridiculous, Pam thought. Snowflakes in the middle of summer?

She peered hard through the glass. Was it snowflakes? It couldn't be, surely? Maybe it was hail.

Pulling back the blind, Pam stared at the fluffy white flakes whipped into frenzy by a stiff breeze.

My goodness, she thought. It is snow. Maybe I ought to nip out for another loaf . . .

She couldn't help chuckling as that thought popped into her head. After all these years, it was still the first thing she thought of at the sight of snow.

She supposed it was because her mother had always thought of it. Shops weren't open all hours during the winters of her childhood, and not many people had freezers back then – though you hardly needed one.

Pam closed her eyes. She was back in 1962 again; a young girl, leaning on the bitterly cold window ledge and staring in awe at the tumbling snowflakes crossing the yellow of the street lamp across the road.

"Snow!" Pam remembered the thrill and excitement that had washed over her on that Boxing Day evening, as she watched the flakes spin in the air.

Lots of wonderful snow to play in – and it was still Christmas! Well, just. There was no school, and if it just kept snowing for a few more days, the schools might close for even longer . . .

Then her father had peered over her shoulder, looked out of the window, and spoiled it.

"It'll just be a few flakes," he said. "It won't settle."

But that year he was wrong. Not only did it continue to snow, but it

kept on snowing, and snowing, and there had been no school. Or anything else, for that matter.

It was countrywide, and all over the news. Frozen pipes and frozen rivers – even frozen sea – and icicles almost down to the ground.

Nearly everything came to a halt, and by the time the weather finally eased, several weeks later, even Pam had to admit she was heartily sick of the white stuff.

It was a little after that, when the snow had finally disappeared and spring decided to arrive, that Andy had moved in on the other side of the street.

She could still picture the removal van now – it was cream with green writing – and the few pieces of furniture, carried in by two men in caps and rolled-up shirtsleeves.

"That's a lovely sideboard," her mother had murmured, glancing over while pretending to weed the garden.

Pam hadn't been interested in sideboards. She was too busy watching a young boy firing a catapult at a tin in his front garden.

His hair was the colour of straw and it stuck up on one side, as though squashed.

One half of his shirt collar protruded from the top of his red jumper like a flag, and his shorts were grubby.

Pam sat on the wooden gate, watching as stone after stone hit its mark and the tin bounced and hopped about as if bitten.

With the last stone, the tin flew up into the air and over the wall,

117

landing on the pavement outside, and Andy hopped over the wall after it.

That was when he looked up and saw her. Forcing the catapult into his back pocket, he walked across the road.

"Hello," he said. "Do you live here?"

"Yes," she answered.

He glanced up at her house.

"Want to have a go with my catapult?"

"All right." She nodded.

Pam chuckled as she remembered the look in Andy's eyes that day, when she'd soundly demonstrated her skill with a catapult. Most boys would have been annoyed that she was such a good shot.

Most boys, she thought, would have said girls had no business being good at catapults.

But not Andy.

He was a tiny bit peeved when her squeezy-bottle boat out-sailed his on the river during the long, sunny days of the school holidays. And he had been a bit put out to find she was good at climbing trees.

But when he fished some chocolate out of his pocket, he still picked off the fluff and offered her a piece.

$$* \quad * \quad * \quad *$$

Over the next few summers, they spent many happy days watching the wildlife from the tree Robin Hood had hidden in when he came down south for a holiday, or swinging their legs in the water from the wooden bridge.

Slowly the years drifted by, and before they knew it, secondary school loomed before them. But in between homework and lessons, they still found time to meet up.

Pam helped Andy with history, art and English, and he helped her with maths, science and more or less everything else.

"Do you know what? I'm going to make a cabinet," he announced grandly one day.

"Are you?" she asked. "That's great. Eddie Marsh has asked me to the pictures. Do you think I should go?"

It was the first time she'd known him to be short of words.

"If you want," he said after a short silence.

Pam hadn't been at all sure if she wanted to go or not, but she'd given it a try, even though Eddie Marsh did smell rather strongly of vinegar.

In those days, everyone knew Eddie's dad owned the local fish and chip shop, so no-one remarked on it. After some thought, Pam had decided it was a small price to pay for all the chips they could eat.

The following week the class was buzzing with the news that Andy had asked Hayley Summers to the pictures, only to receive a rather blunt refusal.

"Does he think I'm daft?" Hayley had squealed to her afterwards. "He wants to go exactly when you're going! Everyone knows he's got a crush on you."

Andy had apparently scurried, red-faced, from the classroom. After a long search, Pam finally found him sitting on the wooden bridge over the river.

"I suppose you've heard," he muttered.

"I heard."

"I thought you were going to the pictures again with Cod-and-chips," he said sourly.

"I was. But his dad wants him to help in the shop."

"Oh. Sorry."

"Bet you could make a better bridge than this," she said, offering him her last piece of chocolate.

"Course," he answered, and took it.

Things settled down again after that.

Then one day, three months later, the gleaming new telephone in Pam's hallway suddenly rang, and kept on ringing, and Pam had a feeling before she'd reached the bottom of the stairs that something was most definitely wrong.

"We're moving." Andy's voice was strained. "Mum and Dad have just told me. We're moving to Yorkshire."

He said "Yorkshire" as though it were Outer Mongolia.

"Yorkshire's lovely," she said. "I've been there for holidays. Mum says —"

"Pam. We're moving." He repeated it as though she couldn't possibly have realised.

She hadn't.

"Moving?"

"What am I going to do, Pam?"

"Meet me at the bridge first thing tomorrow," she said. "Don't worry. We'll think of something."

They met, and they sat and thought for hours, but it was no good.

Six weeks later, they said goodbye.

*   *   *   *

Standing at her window over 40 years later, staring at a freak snowstorm, Pam remembered watching as Andy and his family disappeared into the distance in their new Cortina.

They'd written to each other, of course. Every day at first. Then every week, then once a month, then just occasionally.

She still sometimes felt a little swell of sadness when she thought about it.

She heard the post hit the mat downstairs, and went down to collect it. She was pleased to see the letter she was hoping for: confirmation of a commission for her design business to completely refit and decorate two houses.

The usual circulars were destined for the bin, until a glossy flyer caught her eye. It was decorated in shades of cream and green, and headed *Andy Williamson – Bespoke Carpentry*.

Pam caught her breath.

"Andy Williamson?" she whispered. "Andy? Surely, it can't be."

Of course it couldn't be. She was being silly; it was a very common name.

And yet . . .

It was her daughter, Julie, who finally persuaded her.

"How do you know, Mum?" she asked. "It might be him. And even if it isn't, well, you do still need a carpenter."

Pam nodded, though she strongly suspected that this was another attempt at matchmaking. Since she and Julie's father had amicably divorced, her daughter had been trying to persuade her she needed a new partner.

Pam stared down at the leaflet. Perhaps she had a point. It couldn't hurt to ring the number, could it?

It might be him. And if it was? Well, they were friends, and you never really lose a friend. Not a good friend.

* * * *

Eventually plucking up the courage to ring the number, Pam listened to the voice on the other end of the telephone, and felt the years peel away.

The voice sounded older and deeper, but it was still unmistakeably Andy.

They met again three days later – for the first time in forty-five years – in the oak-beamed cosiness of a tiny pub. It felt as though they'd never been apart.

"So," she said, after they'd exchanged family details and looked at photos. "Do you still have that catapult?"

"You're never going to believe this," he said, smiling. "But I came across it in the loft last weekend. Why did I suddenly decide to sort the loft?"

He gazed at her.

"Who knows?"

* * * *

"Ready, pet?"

Pam felt Andy's arms slide around her waist as he held her close.

They were standing before the same window – the window where only two weeks earlier soft fluffy snowflakes had spiralled through the air, kissing the vibrant heads of the bedding plants.

She turned to face him, still overwhelmed with the love that had seized them both, and together they walked out into the garden.

The sun was shining down, pulsing with the heat of summer; the icy snowflakes were just a memory.

As they stepped on to the bridge, which was draped with garlands of flowers, Pam slipped her hand into Andy's and leaned close to his ear.

"Bet you could make a better bridge than this," she whispered.

"Course," he said, and kissed her. ■

Illustration by Sarah Holliday.

Pumpkin Magic

by Annie Harris

G RANNY! Look what I've got!"

The little girl staggered into the kitchen, her face red with exertion.

"My goodness, Milly!"

Her grandmother glanced up from the cake she was mixing.

"Aren't you strong!" she said, taking the huge orange pumpkin and setting it carefully on the table.

"Yes, and isn't Grandpa clever for growing it?" Milly's grandfather said, kicking off his wellie boots and padding into the kitchen.

"Yes, you are, Grandpa," Milly said seriously. "It's like the giant turnip in that story you read me."

"So it is."

He rooted around in the kitchen drawers for a clean dishcloth, before giving the pumpkin a polish.

"Now, if you move out of our way, Megs, we'll get started."

"Well, let me just put this cake in the oven; it's up to the temperature. Here, this is my sharpest kitchen knife. Be careful with it, Bob — and Milly, darling, you can't help with this bit. You must just watch Grandpa.

"Oh, and remember Jess said to save the flesh — she wants to try making a pumpkin pie."

"Yes. Mummy saw a recipe in a magazine, and she wants to roast the seeds with oil and salt. So we have to save them as well."

"All the innards, then, Milly. We'll have to remember not to throw them in the bin, or you and Mummy will go hungry!"

Her grandfather ruffled her hair, then took up the knife.

"Right, let's get to work, or you'll have to go before we've finished. We'll take his topknot off first, shall we? And that'll be his hat."

Milly sat watching him, wide-eyed, her chin on her hands.

"Cinderella goes to the ball in a pumpkin coach, Grandpa, doesn't she? Daddy read me the story last night. Her fairy godmother made her fetch a pumpkin from the garden, then she tapped it with her magic wand and it turned into a great big coach."

"When your mummy was little, we took her to see a pantomime about Cinderella."

He was carefully scooping out the yellow flesh and putting it to one side.

"She loved it. I remember when the fairy waved her wand and everything went dark, then — hey presto! — there was a beautiful coach drawn by two little white ponies."

"I wish I could see 'Cinderella'." Milly sighed wistfully.

"Well, we're taking you to see 'Jack And The Beanstalk' at Christmas. Granny bought the tickets just last week. But maybe they'll do 'Cinderella' again next year."

"That would be great!"

"Now, can you help me scoop out the seeds for Mummy? Here's a spoon."

"Do you know any more fairy stories, Grandpa?"

Frowning with concentration, Milly was carefully picking out the seeds.

"Well, let me see. I know 'Puss In Boots'."

"Oh, Miss Fletcher read that to us the other day. It's funny."

She giggled and looked across at the large marmalade cat who was curled up on the kitchen window-sill, watching a pair of blackbirds intently.

"Granny ought to make Tiger some giant-size boots."

"I don't think he'd like them, love. He wouldn't be able to walk very easily in them."

Her grandfather finished clearing the pumpkin shell, and began carefully marking out in ink a pair of eyes, a triangular nose and a big mouth full of wicked-looking teeth.

"Anyway, Milly, how about the story of the frog who turned into a prince?"

"When the princess kissed him? I know that one, but I don't like it really. She was horrid to him."

"Well, let me think. Oh, yes." He laughed suddenly. "I'd forgotten all about it, but this pumpkin reminded me."

"Is it a funny story, Grandpa?"

"Yes, it's very funny. Now, how shall I begin? I know – once upon a time there was a young prince."

"Handsome young prince," Milly corrected him. "Young princes are always handsome."

"Oh, yes, of course he was."

"What was his name? Was it Prince Charming?"

"No. He was called Robert."

"Robert?" She looked dubious. "That's a funny name for a handsome prince."

"Well, that was his name, I'm afraid. In any case, there was a very famous king called Robert who once had an adventure with a giant spider."

"Like Incy Wincy Spider?"

"Sort of, yes. But I'll tell you that story another day."

He gathered his thoughts.

"Although young Robert was a prince, he never seemed to have enough pocket money."

"But his daddy was the king!" Milly protested.

"Yes, but this particular king was a bit short of money himself."

"He must have spent it all on buying lots of lovely clothes for the queen, and an extra big crown for himself."

"Probably. So, Prince Robert decided he'd better get a weekend job when he wasn't at college."

"But princes don't go to college," Milly objected again. "They have tew-tors at the palace to teach them how to help the people round about. Ooh, those eyes are really good, Grandpa!"

"Well, be that as it may, on the noticeboard outside the village post office near his house – I mean his palace – the prince saw an advertisement for a young person to help at a nearby farm. So he went there on his bike."

"His bike?" Milly exclaimed.

"Well, his trusty white charger had got a stone in its hoof and was lame," her grandfather amended hurriedly. "The farmer gave him the job and set him to work in a pumpkin field.

"Archie – that was the farmer's name – said he was growing pumpkins for the first time to sell to the local supermarket for Hallowe'en.

"So Robert was put to hoe the weeds between the rows. All the pumpkins were only tiny so far, nothing like this chap here.

"It was quite a big field, and by the time he'd reached the middle, he was getting an awful backache."

"I suppose he wasn't used to hard work." Milly shook her head sympathetically.

"No, he wasn't." Her grandfather laughed. "But then Margaret, the farmer's daughter, came out to bring him his elevenses − a big mug of tea and a chunk of lardy cake.

"She was wearing old dungarees with a hole in one knee, but she was so beautiful, with long hair and deep blue eyes, that she must really have been a princess in disguise."

"So she was Prince Robert's long-lost sister?"

"No, no. Er, she came from another country, far, far away. She was hiding from her wicked stepmother."

"Oh, like Snow White!"

"Exactly. And Prince Robert was going to spend a lot of time in the future wishing he could hide from her, too."

"What, Grandpa?"

"Nothing, love. Anyway." He ploughed on resolutely, before there were any more interruptions. "What do you think happened next?"

"The prince fell in love with her," Milly said promptly.

"That's right − head over heels. And as he watched her walking away through the pumpkin field, he thought to himself: that's the girl − sorry, princess − I'm going to marry."

"So what did he do, Grandpa? Did he tell her?"

"No, he didn't dare. He was a bit shy, but his heart was so full of love that he had to tell someone his secret, so −"

"Oh, look, Grandpa! You've drawn his nose too big!"

"Dear me."

They both studied the pumpkin for a moment, then he took a cloth and scrubbed out the ink to redraw the outline.

"There, that's better. I'm glad you spotted that, love. I was getting a bit carried away with the story."

"So who did he tell?"

"Well, it wasn't a who. It was a what. He took his penknife − he was in the Boy Scouts, you see, and always carried his penknife with him. It was a really good one, and it had a thing for getting stones out of horse's hooves −"

"But it didn't get the stone out of his trusty white charger's hoof, did it, Grandpa?"

"No. Well, that was a particularly big stone." He laughed a little uncertainly.

"What did he do with his knife?"

"He chose a nice little round pumpkin, and on the bottom, where it couldn't be seen, not even by mice, he carved in tiny writing: *Robert loves Margaret XXX.*"

"Ooh, Grandpa. That was naughty!"

Milly giggled.

"Did he make a wish?"

"Oh, yes, he certainly did."

"And if it was a magic pumpkin, his wish would come true!"

"Of course. Everyone knows about pumpkin magic."

"And did it?"

"Well, you'll have to wait until the end of the story. Anyway, Robert carried on working at the farm. Sometimes he helped with the cows, and sometimes he weeded the pumpkin field, because weeds keep on growing."

"Yes, Daddy grumbles about that in our garden."

Her grandfather nodded.

"Of course, he saw the princess every time he was there, but he was still very shy. And although he longed to ask Margaret to go with him to the disco – ball – in the village hall, he couldn't manage it. Because he was so afraid that she would just laugh at him, and his wish wouldn't come true.

"And then, one terrible day, he saw her all dressed up –"

"In a beautiful ball gown?"

"Well, no, but it was a very pretty dress – pink with white spots. And she went off on the back of Jason Hall's motorbike . . . horse. The prince knew that Jason – he was a right little tearaway."

"Oh, no!" Milly cried. "What was the prince supposed to do now?"

"Well, the very next weekend they were planning to gather up all the pumpkins, because they had grown as big as this chap," he said, beginning to carve a grinning mouth.

"So, Prince Robert made up his mind that he would pluck up his courage and ask her out, before Jason could take her away to his cave again, for good this time."

"Jason lived in a cave? Why would Princess Margaret want to go there? Caves are all yucky and dark."

"I really don't know, love," her grandfather said with a wry smile. "It never made much sense to me, either."

"So, did he ask her? Did Prince Robert ask her out?" Milly was hopping up and down excitedly.

"No. Disaster! He caught a bad cold, and his mummy –"

"The queen . . ."

"Yes, she made him stop at home. And when he went the next weekend, the first thing he saw was the farmer's barn stacked high with beautiful pumpkins, waiting for Hallowe'en.

"He was set to work polishing them, so that they glowed like the sun, but the moment the farmer had gone to milk the cows, the princess appeared.

"'Robert,' she told him, 'because you were away last week I had to help gather the pumpkins, and I want to show you something'."

"What was it? Was it nice?"

"Yes, I think so. She took him over to the darkest corner of the barn, and there, tucked away out of sight, was a single pumpkin. She lifted it up, and held it out to him.

"'It's a good job I picked this one,' she said. 'Look.'

"To his horror, he saw that as the pumpkin had grown, his message had grown with it, and it was now huge. Enormous. Giant."

"So it really was a magic pumpkin!"

"Well, there was certainly a bit of magic going on there. And when he saw it, the prince blushed red as fire and didn't know where to put himself.

"But the princess started laughing, and he couldn't help joining in. Then she put down the pumpkin, and he kissed her."

"Oh, Grandpa!" Milly sighed ecstatically. "And then Robert and Margaret got married."

"Well, eventually."

"And they lived happily ever after."

"Yes, they did."

He dropped a kiss on her head.

"They did indeed. Oh, hello, Jess, love," he added, as the kitchen door opened and his daughter appeared. "We've just finished. Haven't we, Milly?"

"Yes – and Grandpa's told me a lovely story about a pumpkin and a prince and a princess."

"'Cinderella', you mean? But you know that one already."

"No, Mummy, this is a different one. They were called Prince Robert and Princess Margaret."

"Robert and –" Jess laughed. "Mum? I think Dad's been telling Milly about the secret message on that little pumpkin."

Her mother ducked back into the kitchen.

"The what, love? Oh!" She laughed. "Did you like the story, Milly?"

"Oh, yes, it was lovely. And they lived happily ever after."

"Of course they did, sweetie."

Jess picked up the grinning pumpkin head.

"Thanks for this, Dad, you've done a brill job."

"Me and Milly. I couldn't have done it without you, could I, love?"

"Well, he'll certainly scare the hobgoblins away on Wednesday. And if this recipe turns out all right, you're invited to a Hallowe'en supper – sausage and mash, and pumpkin pie and cream."

"Sounds great. We'll look forward to that."

"Now, say 'bye bye', Milly. We've got to collect your big brother from football practice."

"Bye! See you on Wednesday."

They waved until the car turned the corner, then turned and went back indoors.

"Mmm. That fruitcake's smelling good, Megs."

"Yes." She grinned at him. "If you're a good boy, Prince Robert, you can have a slice at teatime."

"Why, thank you, Princess Margaret." He dropped a kiss on her nose. "You know, it was the best thing I ever did, that magic pumpkin message."

"Go along with you, you old softie." ▨

Magical Olympic Moments

2004

Middle-distance runner Kelly Holmes had won a bronze medal at the 2000 Games in Sydney, and headed to Athens four years later with her eyes firmly on the podium places.

She brought back not one, but two Olympic golds.

Having been hampered by ill health and injury during training, her moment to shine came when she finished first in the 800 metres. She fought hard for the win, and her incredulous, wide-eyed look when she crossed the line first is the perfect picture of delight and surprise.

The 1500 metres followed, and she ran a controlled race, winning comfortably.

Holmes still holds the records over the 600, 800, 1000 and 1500 metres distances, a testimony to her athletic prowess.

She was appointed Dame Commander of the British Empire (DBE) in 2005, the same year she retired from athletic competition.

Also in winning form in Athens was GB's 4 x 100 metre relay team, comprising Jason Gardener, Darren Campbell, Marlon Devonish and Mark Lewis-Francis.

The team surprised everyone by beating the odds to finish ahead of their USA rivals by one-hundredth of a second – the first British team to win gold in this relay event since 1912. ■

Alamy.

The Apple Dream

by Em Barnard

FLORA tucked her red hair under her cotton cap as Sam bent over, hands propped on his knees. She set a black boot on his back and climbed up on the wall, swinging a leg over to sit astride it.

"Be careful," Sam warned her. "Someone might be there now."

Swinging her second leg over, she jumped down to the ground.

She ducked down and waited, just in case, but it remained peaceful in the two-acre apple orchard.

The weak morning sunlight shining through the branches caused a network of shadows on the dewy grass.

A handful of birds, also raiding the fruit, flew off at her approach.

She had done this before – as had all the children in the village. Ancient Ada had never cared. She would appear, brandishing her stick, but would laugh as they scarpered, and never complained to their parents.

Since she had died and the cottage lay empty, the apples were as bountiful as hedgerow fruit to the children.

This time Flora was determined to pluck apples from the big tree on the cottage-side of the orchard, something too daring for her to have tried before.

She crept up to the tree, keeping her eyes on the cottage. Its upper windows, over a thicket of rambling bushes, appeared dark.

Grasping the lowest branch, she set her foot on the trunk and began to climb. She was after just two apples: one for her and one for Sam.

She selected them and stuffed them in her pinafore pockets – it was all they could hold. But her smile of success turned to a cry of surprise when fingers clutched her collar.

"Will you stop struggling?" a female voice said with a hint of laughter. "I'm not going to hurt you, but I am not letting go, either, until I have your promise that you'll not run off."

Set in 1920

Illustration by iStock.

Flora turned to see a woman in green jumper, brown breeches and boots. Her dark hair was bound under a scarf.

She reminded Flora of the Land Army girls who had worked on the nearby farms during the war.

"I won't run," she muttered.

The young woman released her.

"It was the birds flying up that alerted me. Now, would you like a glass of apple crush?"

"Yes, please, miss."

"My name's Eleanor Cheverton. You can call me Nell, for I'm sure we're going to be friends."

She led Flora into the kitchen.

"It is a mess, but I'm just moving in. I've been tidying some of my grandmother's stuff, to make way for my own few things."

She stepped round a pile of boxes to arrive at a Welsh dresser, then reached for a glass and poured some crush into it.

"The last of it," she said. "Tastes good, eh? It's made from the ruby red apple you've been scrumping. Grandma Ada used to bring us some when she visited.

"She was very protective of the two ruby red trees, for they were planted by her grandfather long before the rest of the orchard. That's why she made sure you children only took apples from the other trees."

"During the war, she gave the other apples to the villagers," Flora said. She tugged the ruby reds from her pocket guiltily.

Nell smiled.

"What's your name?"

"Flora," she replied, twitching her nose at the syrupy sweet smell that seemed to ooze from the walls. Then her eyes widened as they landed on the source of it.

"Ah, you've found me out," Nell said. "That's what I'm hoping to do

– sell toffee apples along with the apple crush."

She went to a tray beside the range, where a dozen of them sat on greaseproof paper under a muslin frame.

"Grandma Ada used to do the same, before the war. Before arthritis crept into the hands. So I have decided that, now I've inherited the cottage, I might do so, too. What do you think?"

"I'd have to try one first," Flora said pertly.

"Exactly why I way-laid you. Take one for yourself and one for your friend who helped you over the wall.

"Now, go out through the gate. We don't want you dropping them climbing that wall."

Within a few weeks, the little business had grown, and Flora eagerly helped after school.

*   *   *   *

Flora passed down a toffee apple to the last child outside the window of the scullery. The delight on their faces always cheered both her and Nell.

She watched the group leave before returning to the kitchen, then she carried on working, twirling another apple into the saucepan of toffee before placing it with the others on the tray and covering them with a muslin frame to keep off insects.

For seven years now she'd been helping Nell in her spare hours, and business was brisk.

Nell stepped in from the outhouse where she had been bottling apple crush and removed her old gabardine coat.

"This is the last of the apples," Flora told her. "I was talking to Fred in the greengrocer's, and he gets apples all year round from a supplier down Barking way. Some big orchard that has a cold store.

"I could get Sam to run us down on Sunday in the pony and trap – see if they'd trade with us, even though we are a small concern."

Nell sank down in a chair, hand on heart to catch her breath.

"I confess, I never expected it to take off like this."

She flung her scarf aside, her dark hair bouncing free, and patted her brow. It was hot in the kitchen with the range on all day.

"And you can't keep on helping me, you know. You should have a proper job, and be earning a decent wage like other girls your age."

"I have got proper jobs!" Flora replied.

"Working part-time at the village bakery and at the greengrocer's isn't enough for you."

Flora smiled at Nell.

"When the right job appears, I'll skedaddle after it. I promise. Now, shall we enquire about the apples?"

*   *   *   *

Flora had been talking to Sam about growing the apple business.

Hands sitting idle in the lap of her summer dress, a wide-brimmed hat shading her face, she glanced over the clusters of primroses and violets that were bursting open along the lane as they travelled in the trap.

She wished Nell had come with them, but she had had letters to write, she informed them.

Flora told Sam she was sure it was a ploy so they could have the day to themselves.

And, to be truthful, her heart swelled not only because of this warm day, but also because Sam was at her side.

He was growing into a muscular man thanks to all that thumping at the anvil in his dad's blacksmith yard. He wore a black waistcoat and trousers, his shirtsleeves rolled up, forearms tanned and sinewy.

They would marry one day, they both knew, even though it was unspoken.

She spotted a frown on his face now.

"Is something troubling you, Sam?"

"Eh? Oh, nothing. Well, yes. It's this apple lark, it can't go on. Don't turn away, Flora. It's fine for Nell – she's secure in that cottage and she can afford to play about."

"It's not playing about! It's a growing concern."

"Where would it grow? It's at bursting point already. And besides –"

"Besides nothing! Without me, Nell wouldn't even have a business. We enjoy it, as well as each other's company."

Flora took a deep breath to curb her temper. Because Sam was right.

She and Nell had talked about their lack of space. But Nell would have to sell the cottage, and it had been in her family for 100 years.

Deep down Flora understood, but she had so many ideas for apples! Chutneys, apple pies, cakes and cider. Sweets, even.

But there was also Sam, and Flora knew her future was marriage and children. No room for a business.

She was stuck between two dreams.

They had cleared a rise to see before them a swathe of apple blossom.

"This looks like the place," Sam said. "I'll leave you to do the talking, but if I think you're being taken for a ride, I'll step in."

Flora kissed him on the cheek.

"Thank you, Sam. And I will think about us. I do love you."

*   *   *   *

"Let's celebrate with a picnic," Sam said as they left an hour later.

"We didn't come prepared," Flora replied, still smiling over her deal.

"I did. I knew you would succeed."

He stepped off the cart and went round to lift her down.

"It was a bit worrying, that. You not needing me."

"I'll always need you, Sam," she replied.

"Is that why you told them you'd collect the apples each Sunday, so we would be together?"

He threw back a cover to lift out a hamper. "They'd have charged extra to deliver them."

Suddenly, she realised it was the wrong answer. But Sam had been teasing, and he was grinning at her.

Thoughts were racing through Flora's mind.

Mabel, the owner of Lea Farm, had been running the business on her own for thirty years, ever since her husband's death in the Boer War.

Her story had opened up Flora's own dream of running a business.

She knew her confidante in this matter needed to be someone out of the village circle. So, when collecting the next batch of apples, and while Sam was busy with the cart, she told Mabel what she was thinking.

Mabel laid a plump hand on Flora's.

"Sometimes, you have to put one dream on hold while growing the other. You're not yet twenty. Saving for your future – be it with Sam, or in business – has to be a choice only you can make."

* * * *

"But that's wonderful, Flora!" Nell said, tipping sugar in a pan.

"Thank you. Sam is delighted. He's running me the four miles to town each day in the trap, just to make sure I arrive!"

She laughed.

"The manageress thought I was after the counter assistant job, but when I told her I was interested in the position of wages clerk, and said that I had cashed up in my two part-time jobs, she took me on."

Flora looked forward to learning how to run a business while working at the women's outfitters in town. She would be earning a good wage, and it would also be the first step on the ladder to becoming as successful as Mabel.

Later, as Sam walked her home from Nell's, she told him about her ambitions.

"Hey, hold up a minute," he said. "I'm not stopping you having your apple dream, but I want mine, too. Which is you as my wife. I thought we had that understanding."

"We do. But we've years ahead to save for both our dreams."

Sam went silent a moment.

"As long as you get your priorities right. First, we save towards our wedding and a cottage of our own."

In exhilaration, she swung her arms round his neck and kissed him.

* * * *

A couple of summers later, on a clear Sunday afternoon, she and Sam were enjoying a picnic on a rise overlooking the countryside.

Both were lying on the warm grass, gazing at the sky. Flora's mind was in the future, for she'd been saving hard, and her dream was growing clearer and closer. She would own a shop in partnership with Nell. "The Apple Range", they'd call it. It would cover the range of food, drinks and sweets that they could make with their fruit.

Sam broke into her thoughts.

"It's time we were married, Flora. We've enough savings between us to put a down payment on a cottage. And I'd like children."

With that, Flora's apple dream was overlaid with another. She saw herself in a cottage, washing and cooking, children round her knees.

The picture wasn't new. It had been born in her childhood, when she played with her dolls. But once she'd seen Nell and Mabel's success, it had been pushed aside by the apple dream.

"So," Sam said, sitting up. "Your silence tells me you don't want to marry me after all." He began packing the hamper away. "I thought I was a little more important than your apples."

"Oh, Sam, you are. But we're still young."

"You keep saying that."

The journey home was taken in uncomfortable silence, as they each held their own thoughts.

As Sam drew the pony to a stop outside Flora's home and helped her down, he looked into her eyes.

"Maybe we've both presumed too much over the years. About getting married. I have dreams, too, Flora. To take over from Dad one day, with you as my wife, and a son to take over from me."

Flora watched him jump back on his cart and drive off.

He hadn't even kissed her.

*　　*　　*　　*

Later that evening, she went to Nell's to help as usual. She wanted to talk to her, but knew Nell would be on Sam's side. So she said nothing. It wasn't long before she realised that Nell was quieter than usual, too.

Suddenly Nell clutched her chest, reaching for the arm of the settee.

"Nell, what is it?"

"Make us a drink, Flora," she said.

As they sat on the settee, sipping their tea, Nell broke the silence.

"I've been keeping it from you because I didn't want to worry you. I saw a specialist in town last week. I . . . have a heart condition."

Flora gasped.

"I shall be fine, as long as I take things easy. In other words, I'm to give all this up."

Flora looked into Nell's tired eyes. Her face looked dragged down. It scared Flora, who had never noticed before.

"But it's not that simple." Nell sighed heavily. "This little income has helped to keep my head above water financially. I'll have no choice but to sell the cottage and get a smaller place. Maybe a flat in town."

"But I thought you were secure, money-wise?"

"When our home was bombed out and my father killed, we were left with nothing. When Ada died, she left me little else but this cottage."

Flora squeezed her friend's hand.

"We'll find you somewhere in the village, close to Sam and me."

*　　*　　*　　*

Walking home along the lane, silent in the moonlight, Flora was still upset over Nell when Sam approached from the opposite direction.

"Nell's got a heart condition," she blurted out, before he could speak.

Sam wrapped her in his arms. She closed her eyes, welcoming his warmth and protection.

"I hope she's giving up the toffee apples at last," he said.

"Yes. And I shan't be taking over. Mabel once told me that if you have two dreams, you may have to put one on hold while you grasp the other. I got it the wrong way round."

She pulled back to look at him.

"Ever since I was a child, my only dream was to marry you and have children. If you still want me, I will marry you tomorrow."

He beamed.

"Of course I do! That's why I came to meet you. I've been through the same heartache, scared you'd agree to part."

As they walked home she told Sam of Nell's reason to sell the cottage.

"I always dreamed Nell would be around to be godmother to our children. We have to see her settled in the village, where everyone can help look after her."

"I hope she can sell the cottage. But what about the apples in the orchard? The trees are weighed down with fruit this year."

"I thought I'd ask Mabel if she would buy them."

"Good idea. We can pop down to Mabel's one evening, then call at the Royal Oak for a meal to celebrate our future together."

*　　*　　*　　*

A month on, as they were delivering the last batch of apples to Mabel, they discussed Nell's cottage.

"When I asked her about the people who had viewed it, Nell wouldn't look me in the eye. I don't think she really wants to sell."

She paused.

"Sam, couldn't we buy it and let her stay with us?"

"Flora, I love Nell as much as you do. But I would like us to have a place of our own."

"That's what I want, too. I wonder how the good Lord is fixed for granting us a miracle."

Mabel hurried down the driveway to meet them, her face beaming.

"Oh, I'm so glad you've arrived. I want to talk to you both."

Inside, they sat across the scrubbed kitchen table.

Mabel snatched an apple from a bowl.

"Recognise it?"

"It's our special ruby red," Flora said.

"Well, it's more special than you know. It's a lost variety," Mabel said. "Crimson Flash. One of my buyers confirmed it. It's very valuable."

She caught the surprise in their eyes.

"It seems nurserymen all over England will pay a fortune for its pips."

"You mean this could make Nell rich enough to stay in her cottage?" Sam asked.

"Oh, yes, easily."

Flora turned to Sam.

"It's the miracle we prayed for! With the money from the apples, and the whole village taking care of her, Nell is sure to be around to be godmother to our children. Just like I dreamed." ■

Magical Olympic Moments

2008

He would go on to be six-times Olympic champion, and Chris Hoy really raised the profile of track cycling with his record-breaking haul, scooping three golds at the 2008 Beijing Olympics alone. This made him the first British Olympian for 100 years to claim three golds at one Games, since swimmer Henry Taylor at the 1908 Summer Olympics in London.

Nicknamed the "Flying Scot", Hoy set a new world record in the team sprint. Britain would dominate the cycling events in Beijing, winning eight gold medals.

The athletes who shone were Nicole Cooke, who won the women's road race; Jamie Staff, Jason Kenny and Chris Hoy in the men's team sprint; Bradley Wiggins in the men's individual pursuit; Rebecca Romero in the women's individual pursuit; Bradley Wiggins, Paul Manning, Geraint Thomas and Ed Clancy in track cycling men's team pursuit; Victoria Pendleton in the women's sprint and, of course, Hoy again in the men's keirin. ∎

Useful Work

by Alison Carter

N OW, what exactly are you doing, husband?"
Cecily Downie came at last to the top of the stairs, ducked through the door of the uppermost chamber of the house and found her husband on his hands and knees.
"Rolly, you won't be able to get back up again," she said. "You know it. Is this more of your marks?"

He was in the middle of the room with the rug folded back, and when he got up it was with an obvious wince.

Rowland Downie suffered from a wearing-away of the joints, and his wife was for ever trying to get him to do less work – particularly work which tested his knees and elbows.

"Jem and Garnet declare they will do no more carving for me, though I command them," he explained. "So it must be me who does it."

"Well, let Jem and Garnet's refusal be a message to you, my sweet man, that there is no point in it. Come down the stairs, have some bread and cheese and enjoy the fire."

It was November 1622, and Rowland Downie was of the strong opinion that the King was about to visit the house.

Cecily doubted it; the master and mistress were abroad in France, and even if there had once been talk of a royal visit – months back, when Sir Worthney had been eager to arrange one – the plan had surely faded.

Cecily worked as cook at South Jevick Manor, and Rowland was steward. The manor was old-fashioned, and small by the standards of the new great houses going up all over England and Scotland, but it was comfortable, and Rowland took immense pride in its upkeep.

"I will have this house ready for His Majesty, should he decide to halt here on any journey, north or south," he said, as he followed his wife downstairs.

"And where might the King be going on this journey north or south?" Cecily asked, smiling to herself. "This manor house is on the road to nowhere, as well you know. It's in a lovely part of Shropshire, but quite separate from anywhere else."

They had reached the first floor, where the larger bedrooms led off a corridor running away to the left. They turned right to a lesser staircase and the servants' quarters.

"Instead of preparing for the King, who creaks as much as you do, Rolly, and remains much at home by all accounts, you ought to be

helping me ready this house for a night of bonfires and revelry."

"I haven't the time," he told her. "I've been –"

"Carving. Yes, I know," she interrupted.

Cecily loved her husband very much, but he was a fool for superstitions. It was almost as bad as his inability simply to stop working and enjoy the ease that a man should take in older age.

The lord and lady of the manor might well be in France until Whitsun – longer, most likely – and, at fifty-six years old, Rolly deserved a rest.

They had five grandchildren, all healthy and lively and living nearby, and, for her part, Cecily liked nothing better than making games for them, or devising entertainments.

Rowland could make a bat and ball out of wood as well as the best craftsman, or quoits even, and he ought to be passing his leisure time on that rather than making witch marks.

Rowland maintained he was protecting the King from evil spirits. Cecily despaired of him. Seventeen years had passed since those dreadful men had tried to blow up the Houses of Parliament, but Rowland lived in fear that this house would be the place in which His Majesty would meet some terrible evil.

"Those gunpowder plotters were known by everyone to be under demonic influence," he argued with Cecily as they continued downstairs.

"You are so old-fashioned, Rolly," she replied. "We're a godly nation

My Tropical Beach

I close my eyes and visualise a
   beach, a warm blue sea,
And me, just lying on the sand
   beneath a shady tree.
It's peaceful; I can stay for hours,
   I'm here on holiday;
I listen to the waves, and breathe,
   And slowly drift away . . .

Then, oh! A bell that makes me
   jump! Alas, I can't complain.
I smile as it occurs to me I've done
   it once again.
I'm not beneath a palm tree; I am
   on a wooden floor . . .
I fell asleep in yoga class – just
   hope I didn't snore!

Emma Canning

now, with no silly business like witches and imps and suchlike."

Yet, despite all her reasoning, he had made Jem and Garnet carve a "V" and an "M" into the stout oak of the mantelpiece in the room where the King would likely sleep, were he to decide to stray 50 miles off the road and visit their little manor.

"It must be 'V' and 'M'. The Virgin Mary can keep anything nasty from coming down a chimney," Roland had assured her. "It is well known that fireplaces are a weak spot for letting in wicked spirits. It's because they are open to the air."

"If you say so, husband," Cecily had said tersely.

She had been hoping for Rolly's help with the bonfire that they were to light behind the kitchen garden. In her opinion, it was the bonfire that they ought to be thinking of. Not witches.

Had the King not declared that every right-thinking Englishman might build a bonfire on the anniversary of the Gunpowder Plot?

But Rowland was intent on making the house "safe" instead. His efforts, and the pain they were causing in his knees, were based on a single, insubstantial comment their master had made while he was packing for the boat to France.

Sir Worthney had mentioned that the King might want to come, true, but that had been wishful thinking, no doubt.

Rowland, though, paid all heed, and so Jem and Garnet had been called away from mending the kitchen and dairy roof to make maze marks called demon traps on the bedposts in the large bedroom.

"I hope His Majesty won't see your demon marks if he visits us," Cecily said. "They might put him off his breakfast."

Rowland was annoyed at this, and explained again that the criss-cross of grooves in the oak was intended to trap malevolent spirits.

"The devils follow the lines," he said, glowering at her, "and they are unable to find their way back out."

"Oh, are they?" Cecily asked, trying not to laugh.

"His Majesty is known to be frightened of witchcraft. He survived a mighty storm at sea which he believed was raised by witches, so that's another reason."

Cecily nodded and gave up remonstrating with her spouse.

"Well, now that I have dragged you out from under the rug, you have time to sit with me and think up games for the night of the bonfire tomorrow. They like blind man's buff, the little ones. We shall have a good warm bonfire to cheer all our hearts and warm all our cockles."

The grandchildren had not visited the manor for some time; there had been a feverish cold amongst them, and they had been kept away for fear of infection.

Cecily had missed them sorely, and as she readied the manor for their arrival she continued to add to her large stock of cakes and tasty things to eat, until the undercook laughed at her.

"I cannot tell what each of them will like," Cecily told her, laughing, too. "Little Mary is now two years old, and they change so much in a few months."

"Still, a feast for twenty seems a little unnecessary," Jennet said, smiling.

She knew that any work for the welcoming of one's family was useful work; she had eight children of her own down in the village.

∗   ∗   ∗   ∗

Rowland kept fussing about the witch marks as he and Cecily waited for the children and grandchildren to come. He grumbled that he had not finished, and yet he was to be interrupted.

It was a bitterly cold day, with a sky the colour of lead. Just as the children arrived, all of them wrapped up warm and borne along the track on a borrowed cart, snow began to fall in huge, soft flakes.

The five children squealed with delight. They jumped down from the cart and ran about like hares, or spaniels chasing hares, all with their tongues hanging out to catch the snow.

"Now, that's too noisy!" Cecily called out. "Your grandfather will say you're bringing the devil among us with all that wildness."

But she was smiling, and Rowland was just coming outdoors as she spoke. Cecily saw utter delight on his face.

It had been a hard winter so far, and he had felt his ailments on the cold nights. He had forgotten the thrill of the family he loved, and had turned in upon himself somewhat.

Now, however, he seemed to come alive.

"Did I not mean to set a hunt for them?" he asked softly, as the children ran about the courtyard collecting snow into balls for a battle. "When they were meant to come for the Feast of St Michael and the Angels, but were ill?"

"That's right," Cecily said. "You had a great bag of things to hide!"

Rowland turned and headed indoors.

Cecily watched him go.

"Don't tire yourself out, husband!" she called.

"Oh, you and your tiring!" he called back, laughing.

An hour later the children had been summoned inside and dried off, and were all over the manor like a plague of locusts.

They shrieked each time they found a tiny carved spinning top, or one of the lead soldiers taken out of Rowland's own childhood store.

There were feathers to find, and even one little galleon carved from a broken spindle.

＊　＊　＊　＊

It was Rowland himself who went outside in the black night to put a torch to the bonfire. Then all of them – grandparents, daughters, sons-in-law, and tired, happy children – sat in the window seats of the largest bedroom and watched the flames lick and spit.

"God save the King," John, husband of their younger daughter, proclaimed.

"Down with plotters!" the oldest boy called out, though he knew the story only from his books, it having happened a full 10 years before his birth.

"What a blaze!" another agreed.

"It is a proper blaze," Cecily said.

She was standing by Rowland, behind the children.

"Now, Rolly, that was a good day's work," she told him.

"I did some excellent carving," he said in reply.

"The witch marks?"

"The galleon, wife. The rattle for the littlest one."

"There is useful work that a body can do," Cecily said, "and there is –"

"Yes, I know, my dear – there is less useful work. At my age, I should perhaps know the difference."

"If the King rides by tonight, he will have all the honey cakes and cold meats he can ask for." She smiled.

"As well as time spent in the merry company of England's best family," Rowland added.

"Except for his own, of course."

"Perhaps." ∎

Benarty, Fife

THERE'S a sleeping giant in the Fife countryside. At least, that's how the 365-metre-high Benarty Hill appears from a distance.

Situated north of the village of Lochgelly, the hill is a prominent local landmark, forming a ridge between Loch Leven and Loch Ore.

It's said that the name is a reference to King Arthur, he of the Round Table; it translates as "Arthur's ridge", adding to the many legends about Arthur's presence in Scotland.

Today, the hill is a favourite place for walkers. The southern slopes are covered in woodland, and the climb is fairly steep, but the panorama from the top is definitely worth it. On a clear day, walkers are rewarded with views over Fife, Loch Leven, the Lomond Hills and the Firth of Forth. ■

Welcome Home

by Teresa Ashby

"WHAT'S wrong, Boots?" Charlotte asked as the dog stared at her with a low growl in his throat.

Perhaps she'd been wrong to think him gentle and friendly. But this seemed out of character for him.

She'd known him for years, and he'd lived with her for the last two weeks.

"Boots," she said again. His tail thumped as he made a strange whining sound.

She took a step towards him and he stood up.

"Get inside the house, Lewis," she said. "Now!"

"Why?" Lewis asked.

"Do as I say, please."

To think she'd all but decided they could keep the dog. What a terrible mistake that would have been.

"I'm going to call PC Cuthbertson," she said. "He'll have to come and take Boots away. We can't keep him, Lewis."

"No!" Lewis cried. "You can't send him away. You promised!"

"I didn't," she protested, ushering him inside. "I promised to think about it, that's all."

* * * *

Boots had belonged to an elderly neighbour, Tim O'Leary.

Charlotte heard the dog barking one day as she was walking past and had gone to investigate, knowing that something must be wrong. She'd never heard Boots bark before.

When Tim didn't answer the doorbell, she squatted down and looked through the letter-box. Her neighbour lay on the floor. Boots was at his side, wagging his tail, one ear standing upright.

He looked relieved that someone had come at last.

A collie cross, Boots was mostly black, with a white blaze on his chest and white paws which looked as if he was wearing boots.

Everyone loved him, and he loved everyone.

Charlotte called an ambulance and the police, and set about looking for a spare key hidden under one of Tim's flower pots. There wasn't one, and a window in the door had to be broken so the paramedics could get in.

The attending police officers told her to wait outside.

"I'm a nurse. Maybe I can help," she said.

One of the paramedics shook her head.

"Too late, Charlotte. I reckon he died as he fell, probably a few hours ago. There's nothing we can do."

Charlotte bit hard on her lip to stop herself crying. She couldn't recall Tim ever looking anything but robust.

He was someone who often helped his neighbours. He'd walked miles in the snow when no-one could get to the shops last winter.

Illustration by Sarah Holliday.

He had seemed unstoppable.

"I'll call the dog warden," a policemen said. "Unless you . . .?"

"You can't let the dog warden take him, Charlotte," Mrs Lawrence called from next door. "It would break old Tim's heart. He doted on that dog. I'd have him, but my cats don't like dogs."

"I'll take him home as a temporary measure," Charlotte said, knowing her son would be pleased. "Perhaps someone in Mr O'Leary's family will take him when they find out what's happened."

"Thank you," the policeman said. "Can I take your name and address, in case the family want to get in touch with you?"

"You'll be lucky," Mrs Lawrence said. "He didn't have any family. None that visited him, anyway."

"We'll see," the policeman replied. "These things have a way of working out. I'm sorry about your neighbour. I'll go and get the dog."

He emerged from the house a couple of minutes later with Boots on his lead. The poor dog looked lost and confused.

"I've put his bowls and some of his food in a bag. There's a cuddly elephant in there, too. I couldn't find a dog bed, I'm afraid."

*   *   *   *

Back at home, Boots followed Charlotte from room to room. He must have been feeling very lost.

"Why don't you go and lie down somewhere, Boots?" she said.

One of his ears pricked up at the sound of his name.

She'd never had a dog, but she knew Boots, and she stroked his soft head.

"You know he's not coming back, don't you?"

Boots cocked his head. Charlotte wondered how much a dog understood about death, and whether Boots was worried about what happened now.

When it was time to pick Lewis up from school, she took Boots with her. He seemed to enjoy the fuss as people stopped to stroke him.

Charlotte had been walking to the school since Lewis was four years old, and no-one had ever spoken to her before.

She wasn't sure if it was because she exuded an air of "keep away", or because they remembered the car accident that had killed Stephen.

It wasn't her fault, but she'd been driving – and guilt had always weighed heavily on her shoulders.

"Boots! What are you doing here?" Lewis cried as he rushed out of the gates. "Did Mr O'Leary say he could come to meet me from school? Can I hold his lead?"

"Boots is going to be staying with us for a while."

Charlotte waited until they were walking along a quiet path before breaking the news of Tim's death. Lewis's face went so pale that his freckles stood out more than ever.

This was his first experience of death, Charlotte realised. He was too young to remember his father's, although he hadn't forgotten his time in foster care while she recovered from her injuries in hospital.

"What will happen to Boots?" he asked tearfully. "Will he live with us now?"

"They're going to see if Mr O'Leary has any family that can take him," she said. "We're just looking after him, like the Jacksons did with you while I was in hospital after the accident."

"But he won't know them!" Lewis protested, his eyes filling with tears of a different kind. "He knows us. We should keep him."

She wanted to tell Lewis not to get too fond of him, or too used to him being around.

"Just don't get your hopes up," she warned.

*　　*　　*　　*

For the next two weeks, Lewis got up extra early to give Boots his breakfast, brushed him every day and took him for walks with his mother.

Charlotte made a dog bed with an old duvet, but during the evenings Boots curled up on the sofa beside her and rested his head in her lap.

At some point during the night he'd go upstairs and jump on Lewis's bed. More often than not she'd go in to wake Lewis up and he'd be fast asleep with one arm slung across the dog, a look of pure bliss on his face.

It was as if Boots had accepted them as his new family.

Then came the moment she'd been both dreading and looking forward

Afternoon Tea

MY neighbours are coming for afternoon tea,
So I need to get baking – they're coming at three!
I've decided on scones after searching my books,
Which have numerous recipes by all the best cooks.

But they all contradict on what gives the best rise,
So the fact I'm confused is not a surprise!
Buttermilk, baking powder and then soda bic,
Self-raising or plain flour – would that do the trick?

And then cream of tartar could be necessary,
Plus I need to decide – cheese, sultana or cherry?
They all claim distinction, but how do I know
How each ingredient will make my scones grow?

So I take a big risk to avoid indecision
And put everything in, all weighed with precision.
Then I mix it all up and roll out the dough
As three o'clock looms – do my stress levels show?

There's a knock at the door; my neighbours come in;
They need feeding up – they look terribly thin!
The scones are consumed without any objection
And to my relief they say, "Simply perfection!"

Sue Moos

to. The policeman knocked at their door.

"PC Jim Cuthbertson," he said. "We met at Mr O'Leary's."

"Of course," she said. "Come in."

As he stepped into the hall, Lewis appeared and gazed up at him in awe.

"This is my son, Lewis."

"Hello, Lewis."

"I want to be a policeman when I grow up."

"That's great, Lewis. We always need upstanding young men like you to join the force."

He turned back to Charlotte.

"I've come about Mr O'Leary. I'm afraid we haven't been able to locate any family, which means there's no-one to make a decision about Boots."

"Please can we keep him, Mum?" Lewis pleaded. He clasped his hands together and widened his eyes. "Please?"

Charlotte tried to harden her heart.

"I'll think about it," she promised. "But don't get your hopes up. I've never had a dog before, and I really don't know what I'm doing. It's a big commitment and . . ."

Before she could say any more, Lewis had thrown his arms around her. She hesitated, then she hugged him back and held him tight.

"I mean it, Lewis. All I'm promising is to think about it."

"I know," he said, his voice muffled, and she knew he was fighting tears.

It would be so easy to say they could keep Boots. He was a lovely dog, friendly and gentle, but Charlotte was out at work all day.

Was it fair to leave the dog alone for long periods of time?

To nine-year-old Lewis it was simple, but there were so many things to consider.

In her head, Charlotte had already decided they couldn't keep him. Her heart was just taking a while to catch up.

Five minutes later, Charlotte saw Jim to the door.

"What if I don't keep him?"

"I'll try to find him a place in rescue."

"It's just that I have to leave him on his own a lot while I work. It doesn't seem fair. Mrs Lawrence takes him for a walk round the block during the day, but I don't know what I'm doing when it comes to dogs."

Jim looked past her to where Lewis was sitting on the floor next to Boots, hugging him.

"Looks like you've been doing a fine job," he said. "With Lewis, too. I was one of the first on the scene when you had your accident. I got the little lad out of the car."

"I was driving," she said.

"I know. I thought I recognised you at Mr O'Leary's, and your name confirmed it. Charlotte, you don't blame yourself for what happened, do you?"

"I was driving," she repeated dully.

"No-one could have avoided that accident," he said. "In fact, you managed to avoid an even worse outcome."

She looked up at him.

"Really?"

"Your driving skill saved your little boy," he explained. "Focus on that. The accident had the potential to kill you all."

No-one had ever put it like that before. The man who had caused the accident was looking at his mobile phone instead of the road. He had walked away unscathed.

"Has Tim's funeral taken place yet?"

"Not yet. I'll text you the details. He'd left instructions in his will, but nothing about the dog."

She said goodbye and looked for Lewis. He'd gone out in the garden with Boots, and was gathering sticks to add to the bonfire they'd been building to get rid of her garden rubbish.

"Let's get that lit while no-one has any washing out."

Now, she went inside to get a lighter, but when she came out and tested the flame, Boots growled softly.

"Don't you like the flame, Boots?"

He seemed tense all over, as if he might spring at any moment.

It felt wrong to be scared of him, but she didn't know how else to feel.

"Get inside the house, Lewis," she said. "Now!"

* * * *

"Why won't he come in, Mum?" Lewis asked as they stood in the kitchen watching Boots sitting beside the bonfire.

They'd tried calling him, but he ignored them, even when offered food.

"I don't know, Lewis. I'm going to have to call PC Cuthbertson," she said. "He'll have to take Boots away."

"No!"

"I'm sorry, Lewis. This isn't working out."

"You can't send him away, Mum." Lewis sobbed. "Please don't. I love him."

"I know," she said. "I love him, too. I'm sorry."

She looked back at the dog and felt a swell of tears. She did love him, impossible and crazy as that sounded.

She had warned Lewis not to become fond of him, but hadn't she gone and done just that?

Jim wasn't in uniform when he came back. He must have been on his way home when he'd called in earlier.

"You're off duty," Charlotte said. "I'm so sorry."

"Not a problem. What's up?"

"Boots is acting strangely. He won't come in. He's normally so obedient. I had no idea he was so unpredictable. And that's dangerous in a dog, isn't it?"

They went out into the garden, and Jim approached Boots slowly.

"What's up, boy?" he asked.

Boots growled softly again. It was almost like a whisper.

"That's not a growl, Charlotte. Not in any aggressive sense. He's just talking."

Boots wagged his tail as if he knew what Jim was saying.

"You're not going to shoot him, are you?" Lewis asked.

"What? No, never! Boots has a reason for behaving like this. We just have to work out what it is. How long has the bonfire been there?"

"We've been building it for a while," Charlotte said. "Why?"

"I think we may have to unbuild it. He seems to be guarding it for some reason. It's all right, Boots. Don't worry, boy."

The dog watched closely as they began to dismantle the bonfire, twig by twig.

"Don't touch him, Lewis," Charlotte warned.

"Lewis is in no danger," Jim said. "I know dogs, and believe me, Boots doesn't have a mean bone in his body. I think I may be about to prove it to you. Here we are."

He stepped back and lowered his voice.

"It's a hedgehog. Mr O'Leary had several hedgehog shelters in his garden. Boots must have recognised the scent.

"We need to make a safe hideaway for this little fella. We'll cover him back up carefully for now, and I'll come round tomorrow with some wood and sort out something safer. If you don't mind, that is."

"I don't mind at all," she said. "It'll be lovely to have hedgehogs living in the garden. Oh, Boots, I'm so sorry. You were just stopping me from making a terrible mistake."

He licked her ears as she bent down to make a fuss of him, and she felt a strange squeezing sensation in her heart.

She looked up to see Lewis watching her.

"Yes," she said. "He can stay."

She had a lot to learn about dogs, like when a growl wasn't a growl.

"Have you had anything to eat yet?" Jim asked. "I was thinking of getting myself a take-away. I could get us all something."

"Yes, please," Lewis said eagerly.

"That's settled, then." Jim grinned.

*   *   *   *

A few days later they attended Tim O'Leary's funeral together. The crematorium was packed, and they had permission to take Boots along.

The dog was quieter and more dignified than ever. He sat silently beside Lewis, and when Lewis cried, Boots gently nuzzled at his hand.

Jim had come along with them for moral support, and also because he said he felt as if he knew Tim, although he'd never met him.

There was no official wake afterwards, but several of them gathered at a nearby pub to toast Tim's memory.

Later, Jim walked home with Charlotte, Lewis and Boots. When they passed Tim's house, Boots stopped and looked through the gate towards the front door. It was as if he was saying his own goodbye in his own way, and, after a few moments, he heaved a sigh and walked on.

There was a jaunty spring in his step as Lewis ran along with him. By the time they turned in at Charlotte's house, Lewis was giggling.

Boots went in first and sat at the front door, waiting to go in.

"He knows he's home," Jim said, and Charlotte felt a rush of happiness, as if Stephen was watching and nodding his approval.

She imagined Tim standing at her late husband's side, his hand on his shoulder, also smiling. It was just a fleeting image, but it was incredibly comforting.

"Come in, Jim," she said. "I'll make dinner. You're welcome to stay."

"Please stay," Lewis added.

"That would be lovely," Jim agreed, and as they stepped into the house Boots let out a joyful bark. ■

Magical Olympic Moments

2012

Danny Boyle set the scene for a spectacular Olympics with an amazing opening ceremony. Who can forget that moment when James Bond (aka Daniel Craig) escorted the Queen from Buckingham Palace so that "she" could parachute into the stadium? On "Super Saturday", British sporting prowess shone at its brightest. It made for edge-of-the-seat viewing for the nation, let alone for those lucky enough to be in the stadium. And what better place for it to happen than at the home Games in London?

Heptathlete Jessica Ennis, long jumper Greg Rutherford and distance runner Mo Farah all struck gold on that magical night in August. Ennis attained a series of personal bests to command the field, while Rutherford leaped into the history books with an 8.31m jump – the last British man to win gold in this event was Lynn Davies back in the Tokyo Olympics of 1964.

Completing the trio of sporting treasures was, of course, Mo Farah. He became the first Brit to win gold in an Olympic 10,000 metre final. Of course, Mo then went on to claim gold in the 5,000 metres, making him a double Olympic champ, and no-one looked more surprised than modest Mo himself! ■

Playing House

by Meg Hudson

O H, come on, Jane. What little girl wouldn't love a Wendy house?" My dad's shoulders slump and I immediately regret my words.

"You were coming up to five when I made yours," he continues. "It was the first one I'd ever done. It was a bit ramshackle, but you were never out of it. Clare's will be the fifteenth."

"I know, Dad, and I loved it. It was my palace. It was my favourite thing for years."

"You spent every moment you could in there. Even when you started school, you virtually lived in it at weekends and holidays. Your brother's girls are nearly teenagers, and they still love theirs.

"Why wouldn't Clare like one? I don't get it."

"She would, Dad. I'm sure she'd love one," I say. "Just ignore me."

Sadly, I can't ignore my inner voice which is telling me that Clare will love it for half an hour at most, then she'll come bouncing back out and go shinning up the apple tree, or digging up worms and singing to them.

Dear little Clare. She never has toed the girly line. Her blonde hair and blue eyes can't hide the fact that dollies, pink stuff and playing house are not in her repertoire.

She's much more likely to be found throwing herself around outside, climbing up things, falling off things, and endlessly following me about in the garden, "helping".

She likes to help with dead-heading and weeding, though she doesn't always succeed in removing the actual dead bits. Or the actual weeds.

She was three when she found that opened packet of radish seeds at my dad's and scattered them willy-nilly over the crazy paving.

Two weeks later, when we were round there for Sunday lunch, she came bursting in from the garden.

"Grampa! My radishes is comin' up!"

Her radishes had grown to a respectable size in those two weeks, and

Illustration by iStock.

Clare was so happy and so proud that we had no choice but to lift the paving stones in order to pull them out and eat them.

They were good, too.

There is nothing that keeps her indoors. No kind of weather troubles her in the least.

If I tell her it's too cold to be outside, she'll tell me that she plans to put two coats on.

I do see the logic, and I can't help respecting her hardiness.

Clare has never once asked for a Wendy house, never shown any interest in the pink and purple plastic ones her friends like, and has never been seen in the splendid wooden one her grandpa built for her cousins seven years ago.

So you see my dilemma. I don't want to disappoint my kind, lovely, talented dad by talking him out of this, but he'll be more disappointed when he's made a majestic garden retreat with Clare's name on it, and it stands there unvisited while she turns cartwheels on the grass.

What can I do? He's proud of his Wendy houses, and he has always insisted on treating all his grandchildren the same.

There's no choice really: I'll just have to follow the path of least

resistance. I start back-pedalling like mad.

"You're right, Dad," I say. "She will love it. But it's only two weeks till she's going to be five; can you build it in time?"

My dad's face lights up.

"Of course I can, Jane. It's half done already. It's going to be a real beauty."

He's glowing with happiness and excitement. And me? I have a sense of doom.

Two weeks later he brings Clare's house round in his friend's pick-up truck. It's the night before her birthday. She's fast asleep, hugging Foggy, her favourite soft toy.

Together, my dad and I set up her house at the bottom of the garden, alongside the end fence. It really is a thing of beauty.

His skill and eye for detail have got better with every one he's made. Any little girl would be dazzled to wake up to such a wonder on her birthday.

Too bad Clare isn't "any little girl".

We have supper when we've finished, and Dad sleeps in the spare room. He says he can't wait to see her face when she goes out into the garden in the morning.

152

The Visitor

THERE is a little hedgehog
Who comes to visit me,
He likes beef-flavoured cat food,
And meal worms for his tea.

I don't expect repayment
Or even hedgehog hugs –
But how I wish he'd hurry
And eat up all the slugs!

Hazel Mary Martell

I'm relieved he has to leave straight after breakfast to get a good morning's work in on the allotment while the weather's fine.

I know my daughter – there are new chickens in the field beyond the garden wall, and she'll be trying to climb over and gather them round for a chat, all birthday gifts forgotten.

My heart's in my mouth when he blindfolds his giggling granddaughter and leads her down the garden.

I needn't have worried. As he removes the blindfold, Clare squeals with delight and goes running up the three shallow steps into her little house, with its white panels and apple-green door.

"I love it. Thank you!" she yells, running back out and hugging him around the knees, then hurtling back in again, pausing only to gather a couple of snails to keep her company.

I realise I've been holding my breath, so I take a couple of deep, calming ones and head indoors to finish my coffee.

"There, Jane. What did I tell you? I knew she'd love it," my dad says, putting his cap on. "I'll be off now, love."

And he's gone, off to plant out the tomatoes and thin out the salad seedlings.

After I've waved my dad off, I take a peek out of the kitchen window.

Clare has brought one of the spoons her grandpa's supplied for her "parties" out of her house and into the garden.

With unbreakable concentration, she's busily digging up the flower border.

Still, I'm pleased when I see Clare tootling happily in and out of her house for the rest of the day.

When I take a picnic lunch out for us to share, I see that she has filled the shelves and window-sills with stuff from the garden – flowers, buds, snail shells, feathers, some tiny unidentifiable bones.

"Treasure," she says.

"I love my house, Mum," she says that night, as she's dropping off to sleep.

"I love it, too," I say, and I breathe a sigh of relief.

To my great surprise, she spends an idyllic two days sorting her treasures and setting them out neatly in her house.

And then – nothing.

The natural world is calling her, and her beautiful Wendy house is forgotten. She's back out in the garden full-time, rolling about on the grass, blowing dandelion clocks, live-heading the pansies.

I want to be able to tell my dad that Clare uses her lovely house every day. I try all sorts of temptations. I stock it with her favourite games, and suggest she asks her friend Thomas over to play in her house. She's delighted with the idea.

When Thomas arrives he's amazed by the house, but she's hauled her games out on to the lawn. I can see his eyes returning to it again and again, but Clare's life is in the great outdoors.

I suspect Thomas is a little disappointed. It isn't only girls who like playing in kid-sized buildings.

I invite her older cousins, Belle and Lucy, to come round for a picnic in her new house. Clare insists they're too tall, finds an old sheet to spread on the grass, and carries all the food outside.

I bring her paint box and paper in, and ask her to paint me a picture.

"OK, Mum," she says. "I'm going to paint the chickens, so I'll have to sit on the wall."

Out she goes with her paintbrush.

I give up. I wonder if she'll use it more in the winter, though "Clare Two-Coats" has never been known to be fazed by weather, so it's a bit of a pipe-dream.

Clare's outside when my dad comes to visit, hauling my watering can about and trying to water the container plants, in spite of her diminutive size. She has her own toy watering can, but she prefers mine.

I make tea, and together Dad and I sit and watch her for half an hour as she potters about the garden.

I don't go outside with him when he goes to greet her. I don't want to hear the conversation. I think my heart may break as I watch them, heads together on the bench, talking very seriously.

"You were right, our Jane," he says later. "A Wendy house isn't the thing for Clare, is it? She's bracingly honest."

"I'm sorry, Dad. She's an outdoor girl. She doesn't want to be inside. Even in her own little house."

"I know, love."

He brightens.

"But I know what she really would like. Can you take her out for the day tomorrow?"

So next day, Clare and I take ourselves off to my brother's, and we have a big family picnic in their local park.

It's a fine day, and we stay out for ages. At around five o'clock, I get a text from my dad with a thumbs-up icon.

"Hi, Grampa," Clare says, surprised to find him there when we get back.

"Hello, Clare. I've got a surprise for you. It's in the garden," he says.

"Are you going to blindfold me?"

Dad laughs.

"If you like."

"No," Clare replies. "It's OK. I'm just going to go and look."

Seconds later, we hear a loud cry and she bursts back into the kitchen. She jumps up on to her grandpa's lap and hugs him tightly, then grabs me by the hand.

"Mum, come and look. Look what's in the garden."

She's so excited she can barely get the words out. She drags me down the path to the bottom of the garden.

"Look what Grampa made me!"

She lets go of my hand and runs inside.

My dad has removed the wooden panels from the walls and roof of the Wendy house and replaced them with plastic "glass". He's built shelving along the walls, and brought seedlings, little flowers and tomato plants from his greenhouse.

There's a bag of potting compost, a trowel and a small, but real, watering can.

"What do you think, Clare?" my dad asks.

"Oh, Grampa. It's my own greenhouse!"

*　　*　　*　　*

I've hardly seen Clare for the past few weeks. She's eager to learn, and my dad comes over most weekends to share his expertise with her.

He's cleared a small plot near the greenhouse for her outdoor vegetables. She's learned how to plant out her greenhouse-grown tomato plants at the right time, how to thin out seedlings, and all about growing tender plants under glass.

Today she's been to the allotment with him, digging up potatoes; she can't wait to grow her own crop of spuds.

"These are for our dinner. They're Grampa's," she says, plonking a bag of potatoes on the kitchen table.

"And these radishes are for pudding. I grew them myself. I think we'll all have dinner in the greenhouse today."

It's a bit of a squash! ■

Red, Red Roses

by Toni Anders

NOT again," I grumbled to myself as I reached the porch of my house. There was an almond-pink box propped up against the door.

I didn't need to read the green, spidery writing scrawled artistically across the box. I knew what it would say.

Phillippa's Flying Flowers.

"He said he'd sort it out," I muttered, carrying it into the house.

The first box had arrived last week. My initial reaction, on seeing it, had been excitement.

The label had been correct. It was certainly my address: Pine Tree Cottage. But who would send me flowers?

I'd finished with Gary three months before, and since then there'd been no-one else.

I'd opened the box and lifted out a beautiful bouquet of red roses, perfumed and velvety. Red roses – the symbol of love.

I'd laid them carefully on the table. Did I have a vase worthy of red roses?

Then something had made me glance at the label again. There was a gap above the address, then the name.

Mrs Coral Blakemore.

Coral Blakemore? My name was Jasmine Forester.

The flowers were not meant for me.

I'd sunk into an armchair and looked at the box.

I'd felt cheated. For half an hour I'd had the exciting feeling that I had a secret admirer.

I'd lived in the cottage for only six months, and knew few of the neighbours. I'd never heard of Coral Blakemore.

But Millicent would know her. Millicent lived opposite and knew everyone.

She was not a busybody, just one of those people who was interested

in everything and knew everyone.

I'd dialled her number.

"Coral Blakemore," Millicent had mused. "Ah, yes. She lives ten – no, twelve doors down from you. The house with blue striped curtains.

"When I say lives, she's actually staying there at the moment with her brother, Peter."

I knew Millicent would be dying to know why I wanted Coral Blakemore. I'd satisfy her curiosity next time we met. I thanked her and rang off.

Well, there was nothing for it. I'd have to take the box to this lucky Mrs Blakemore. The flowers would soon need water.

The house had been easy to find. When I'd seen the name on the gate, I'd realised the possible reason for the mix-up.

It was Elm Tree Cottage.

I'd rung the bell.

The door had been opened almost immediately by a tall young man with dark hair and devastatingly blue eyes. I'd explained the reason for my visit and handed over the box.

He took it and sighed deeply.

"It's for my sister. Thank you for your trouble. I'll give it to her when she comes in and ask her to sort it out."

Why the deep sigh, I'd wondered, as I made my way back up the road. Perhaps he didn't approve of his sister's admirer.

*   *   *   *

That had been three days ago, and now a similar box was waiting on the doorstep. I marched straight down to number twenty-four.

The same young man answered my knock.

"Not again!" he said, as he took the box. "I'm so sorry. I asked her to sort it out."

"It's quite all right. It's no trouble," I said untruthfully.

"Look, would you like to come in for a coffee?" he asked. "We're neighbours, and now we've met we should get to know one another."

Why not? It was one way to get to know a neighbour. And, as far as I could see, he was quite a desirable neighbour.

The sitting-room was cluttered with magazines, shoes, DVDs and handbags. For a moment he looked embarrassed.

"I'd forgotten Coral's mess," he apologised. "She always was an untidy little madam, even as a small girl. I don't spend my time in here; the kitchen is my domain."

We went into the kitchen, which was neat, clean and organised.

He had one of those expensive coffee machines, and almost immediately presented me with a cup.

We sat at the breakfast bar.

"I'm Peter Cayley," he said, holding out his hand.

"Jasmine Forester."

I grasped his hand. It was warm and smooth.

"How long have you lived in Pine Avenue?"

For the next ten minutes we swapped information about ourselves and our lives. He was a draughtsman who worked from home; I told him I was a manager at a doctor's surgery in town.

"Your sister lives here with you?"

"Correction – is staying with me, and slowly driving me mad," he replied, with a rueful smile. "I love her to bits, but she's so untidy and doesn't seem to care."

"So how long is she staying?"

"I wish I knew. She's been married for a year. They're madly in love, but they argue all the time. She swept out after the last row and ended up here.

"The flowers were from Drew, her husband. He's desperate for her to go home, but she just ignores him.

"I wish I could think of some way to persuade her. The trouble is, she won't meet him or talk to him."

I thought for a while.

"Would you like me to help you? I've had an idea."

"Would I? Please!"

"What time does she get home from work?"

"Five o'clock."

"And Drew?"

"I'm not sure. About the same, I believe."

"Right. We'll do it on Thursday night. That gives me two days to prepare."

"Do what? Prepare what?"

"I'll tell you on Thursday afternoon," I said mysteriously. "I shall take the afternoon off and bring everything down at about three o'clock.

"Your job will be to tidy the room, set up a table and two chairs and make sure Drew arrives here before your sister."

The look Peter gave me was a mixture of amusement and bewilderment.

"I don't know what you're up to, but if it works and Coral goes home, I shall be eternally grateful."

✳   ✳   ✳   ✳

On Thursday at three I arrived on his doorstep, carrying two large baskets.

In one was a chicken casserole, cooked and only needing reheating. In the other lay prawn cocktails, and the ingredients for a complicated but delicious sweet for two.

Peter had worked wonders with the room. Gone were all the magazines, shoes and other clutter.

A coal fire burned gently, and in the middle of the room were a small table and two chairs.

I spread a gleaming white cloth and sent him to the kitchen for cutlery. In the middle of the table, I placed the bouquet of red roses.

I handed Peter a bottle of white wine, and he put it in the fridge to cool.

We placed the casserole in the oven, the prawn cocktails on the table, and I assembled the chocolate and raspberry dessert.

It was half past four. I looked with satisfaction at the little table. No girl could fail to be impressed with our romantic supper for two.

Peter looked at his watch.

"Four thirty. I told Drew to be here before five."

As he spoke, there was a ring at the door. Peter rushed to open it.

Drew was fair-haired and stocky, very pleasant and friendly. Peter showed him what we'd done.

"It's all ready. Jasmine has prepared everything."

Drew gave me a beautiful smile.

"It's so kind of you to help."

Coral must be mad to risk losing such a lovely man, I thought.

I explained about the food, then picked up my coat and bag.

"A quarter to five." Peter checked his watch again. "She'll be here soon. I'll be at Jasmine's house if you need me. Here's the phone number."

I'd prepared the same meal for us, but of course the table didn't have red roses.

"Fantastic," he said as he tucked into his prawn cocktail. "I'm so pleased these are back in fashion. I was feeling envious of Drew."

We were both rather shy at first and didn't talk much. Events seem to have moved so fast in the last few days.

But as the meal progressed we began to chatter like old friends. We seemed to have a lot of interests in common, like sketching, running and going on cruises.

We finished our meal. Peter insisted on making the coffee.

"You've worked hard," he said as he handed me a cup of coffee and joined me on the couch.

We sat gazing into the fire.

"I wonder how things are going." Peter voiced what we both were thinking.

"What time will you go home?" I asked.

"Late," he replied. "Give the plan time to work." Then he looked up. "That is, if you don't mind."

I smiled.

"As you say, we must give the plan time to work."

I realised I didn't want him to go.

He looked across the room at a table in the window.

"A jigsaw! I haven't done one of those for years. May I do a bit of it?"

We sat together in front of the picture, and for the next hour were engrossed in the puzzle.

Another interest we have in common, I thought.

At eleven, he pushed back his chair and stood up.

"I must go and see what's happened. I'll phone you."

"This has been a most unusual day," I said, as we walked together to the door.

He put his hands on my shoulders.

"A most enjoyable day," he corrected, and bent to kiss my forehead. "I'll phone," he promised again.

I hadn't long to wait.

"It worked," he said, with an excited laugh. "Drew left a note. They've gone home together."

"So, you've got your house back?"

"Thanks to you. Jasmine, I can't tell you how grateful I am. Will you let me take you to dinner tomorrow?"

* * * *

The next day there was an almond-pink box on my doorstep. The name and address were correct.

Miss Jasmine Forester, Pine Tree Cottage.

I didn't need to open it to know it would contain a bouquet of red roses. ■

Magical Olympic Moments

2016

When the Team GB women's hockey team headed to Rio, they probably didn't dare dream of coming back with gold.

But four years previously they'd managed to win bronze, and the ladies were determined to better that.

They were in impeccable form in Brazil, winning every one of their games on the way to the final.

However, following a 3-3 draw with Netherlands, it all came down to the wire and a dramatic penalty shoot-out.

Keeper Maddie Hinch kept her cool, pulling off some remarkable saves, with Helen Richardson-Walsh and Hollie Webb finding the back of the net to defeat the defending champions.

For the first time ever in women's Olympic hockey history, Britain secured gold.

Rio was Britain's most successful Olympics. An incredible 130 athletes returned home with a medal, including Andy Murray, who defended his Olympic title in an exhausting five-setter with Juan Martín del Potro. In the process he became the first player, male or female, to win two gold medals in a tennis singles event.

Britain managed to increase its magnificent medal haul from its home games four years previously, collecting 27 gold, 23 silver and 17 bronze medals — too many sporting heroes to mention them all. ■

Alamy.

The Strength Of Love

by Em Barnard

J ENNY was floating on air for the first time in over two years. She set the phone down and beamed at her mum beside her.

"Brian's home! He wants to see me. Now."

"I'm pleased he's home safely, love."

Jenny flung her arms around her mum.

"I'm sorry for being horrid to you at times, it was just that I was –"

"I understand, remember? Now, stop clinging to me and go and cling to Brian."

Jenny giggled and kissed her cheek.

"I must change into my navy and white polka-dot dress. He loves me in that one." She thudded up the stairs. "And I'll call and tell Gran on the way to the park."

She burst out her news as soon as Gran opened the front door. In the hall they hugged.

"I'm just happy to see you happy, Jenny," she said as they pulled back and gripped hands.

"I am. I know you kept telling me this wasn't even a war, like those that took Dad and Grandad," she said. "But I was so scared it was going down a third generation. There have been soldiers killed."

"No need to put yourself through it any more. Just go and meet him. And give him our love, too."

Jenny kissed her.

"Thanks, Gran. For understanding." She swept off through the doorway.

She reached the park bench which was so special to her and Brian. His two-year stint in the National Service was over!

She jiggled impatiently as she waited for him on the park bench. He was going to propose; he'd promised that before he left.

And she'd say yes. For the important and only thing that mattered was that she loved Brian, deeply and unceasingly.

She knew he loved her totally, too. He'd told her so many times and in

Illustration by Kirk Houston.

so many ways. The passion in his eyes, the way he touched her cheek, the sensitivity in his voice.

They'd met four years ago. He was passing through his mum's corner shop on his way to meet his mates when his mum hailed him.

"Do something useful, Brian. Help this lady home with her shopping."

His face was sullen with annoyance when hefting up her heavy basket, but he did open the door for her.

"It's for Gran," Jenny told him to break the silence as he marched them along. "She's none too well."

"I haven't got a gran. The only one I'd known died in an air raid when I was five."

"I hate war. It killed my dad, and Grandad in the Great War. But it's been over for years now."

She tried to catch his eye with a smile, to penetrate his sullenness. She saw him suppress a smile, then submit.

"We're playing footie against the Ripley lot on Saturday. Want to come?"

"I'd love to," she fibbed.

He turned and smiled, and her heart somersaulted. After she'd joined the girls and the winning team in celebration, he asked her out often.

One of her regular errands was walking her auntie's tots to the park in the twin-hooded pram.

"I've a favourite bench, between the rhododendrons," she told him, leading him there. Once seated, she sat rocking the pram. "Do you like babies? I want lots of them."

The Times They Are A-changing

TIMES have to change
But I'm being left behind:
These new-fangled things we have
Muddle my mind.

Kindles and laptops;
iPads, pods and phones;
I can't understand them –
Do you think I'm alone?

Once, we wrote letters.
No need for that now.
Texting's so easy –
That's if you know how!

Don't bother with shopping,
Just order online.
Browse Google and Yahoo
With your extra time.

Surf the net, Twitter,
Log in and download.
Dongle, Skype, Snapchat:
Sounds like a code.

In buses and trains,
In shops, in the street
You must have a smartphone
To make you complete.

Technology's great,
But for me, in the end,
I prefer a good cuppa
With "The People's Friend".

Thelma Moss

He looked into her eyes.

"If I find the right girl I want lots of them, too."

In that moment friendship stepped aside for love.

But they were only fifteen. From school he went as apprentice to a cabinet maker and Jenny into a typing pool.

They never saw beyond their little world when it came to romance, but then he turned eighteen and everything changed.

"I don't know where I'll be sent," he told her, regarding his stint in the National Service.

"I hate war."

"I have to go."

She stared at him.

"You could be killed."

He wrapped his arms around her.

"No. I'm too pig-headed to let anything happen to me."

From the training barracks to the Suez Canal, where he'd been posted, he wrote jauntily, leaving out the harsh reality of it, leading her to believe he was unafraid and safe.

But she'd known differently. She'd learned through her mum and gran all about the horrors of war and the loss of a true love.

* * * *

"Jenny!"

She jumped up and they bumped together, crushing into each other's arms.

"I've missed you so much," he told her as she was telling him, too.

They pulled apart, both laughing, and then calmed and sat on the bench, clutching hands.

He hadn't changed – no weary-worn face; just as smiling as she'd remembered him. She relaxed.

She noticed he was wearing his dark Sunday suit, and the red silk tie she'd bought for his eighteenth birthday.

He looked at her, becoming serious.

"You know what I want to say, but I need to tell you something." He paused, his expression anxious. "I want to make the Army my career."

The words echoed in her head.

"No! Oh, Brian, you can't mean it."

"I didn't expect to enjoy it like –"

"Enjoy? How can you say that?" She struggled to free her hands, but he gripped them tight. "You know how I hate war!"

"Jen, it's not so bad. It's a peacetime Army now."

"For how long?" When he stuttered over that unknown answer, she jumped up. "I'll never marry an Army man!"

She ran from him, tears stinging her eyes.

* * * *

Twenty minutes later Jenny knocked on Gran's door.

"What is it, Jenny? Surely he turned up? Come and sit down."

They sat on the sofa in the back room. Jenny was calmer now.

"He wants to . . . to stay in the Army."

Gran twisted her mouth in thought.

"Has he asked you to marry him?"

"It never got that far. I ran away. What am I going to do? You only had Grandad a few months; Mum only had Dad a year. I've stood it for two years. I can't carry this fear every day."

"What about the fear inside Brian every day?" Gran asked gently. "Oh, yes, it's there, Jenny. But he wants to do something about it so you and your children, and other families, don't live in fear of an enemy invading your home. He wants to serve and protect his country.

"If you love him as much as I know you do, you'll serve him by loving and protecting him when he comes home tired and hurting. I never let your grandad down by running from his proposal when war was imminent. And your mum kept her fear out of sight, sending your father off with a smile."

Gran's voice softened.

"Millions of women the world over must carry this burden for our men. It's how we stand beside them in helping to protect this country." She gave Jenny a hug. "I'll put the kettle on."

Jenny stared after her gran. She'd expected comfort and had received criticism.

She considered the two women in her life. Though they'd both lost their true loves, it had strengthened them, especially when they spoke, with pride, of their man's sacrifice.

She couldn't let them down; couldn't be the coward of the family. Yes, she was young, but one day she'd be older like Mum and Gran and she wanted their resolve, their spirit.

She wanted the children that she and Brian would have in the future to be proud of both of them, and safe. And above all that, she wanted Brian.

* * * *

A knock on Gran's front door made her jump.

"Jenny, will you see who it is, please?" Gran called.

Jenny composed herself as she walked down the hall. She opened the door.

"Jenny, please!" Brian reached out a hand in appeal. "I can't let you go like this. I can't let you go at all."

She grasped his hand, stepped forward and cupped his cheek.

She spoke with a strength and calmness she'd drawn from the depth of her being, passed down to her by those stalwarts in her life.

"There's nothing more to say, Brian. I'll follow you to the ends of the earth, because I love you stronger than any war can tear apart," she vowed.

As his lips fell on hers, she knew she was safe.

Whatever the future held for them, she'd be his strength, and he hers. ∎

Stafford, England

ONCE a hermitage on a crossing-point of the River Sow in around AD 700, Stafford grew to become the fourth-largest town in Staffordshire.

Its pottery-making history dates back to AD 913, with a fortified settlement there producing Roman-style ware. The Norman conquest put an end to most industrial activity for many years, but Stafford again became a thriving market town in the Middle Ages.

It was home to many influential people throughout its history, like the famous playwright, Sheridan. Today Stafford presents a pleasing mix of ancient and modern. ■

Out Of The Dark

by Kate Finnemore

I PULL up the collar of my black overcoat to meet the brim of my hat, open the door to the outside – and yelp, as something dark and bulky sags against my shins.

"Percy! Bring the lantern. Quick!"

My breath is shredded white ribbons in the icy air. A single snowflake zigzags slowly down to the ground. It's Christmas Eve, and the church bells are ringing, calling people to midnight mass.

The moon comes out from behind the clouds, and I make out the pale oval of a face against a shadowy mass of shawl and skirts.

My heart trips into a fast, shallow beat. A woman. It's a woman, lying motionless on my doorstep.

Percy pushes past me and holds the lantern above our heads.

"Her! She was in the shop earlier. Begging. Mumbling something, over and over. I told her to clear off."

"We can't leave her here, Percy. She'll freeze to death."

He sighs heavily, a sound that's part anger, part resignation, and puts the lantern down.

He knows I'm a soft touch; that I'll insist we take her in. For this one night, if nothing more.

"Help me lift her up, then, Grace, and get her inside."

Help. I ponder the word as I bend, fumbling and groping through the thickness of the shawl for the woman's arm.

I pull one of my gloves off and touch the woman's cheek. It's icy cold. My fingers bunch into the shawl.

"Her clothes are wet, Percy. She's as cold as ice. We must hurry."

"Looks like we won't be going to church, after all."

"No." I don't mind. I'm not sure I believe any more, anyway.

Percy looks at me. His face is just visible in darker shadows all around. "Ready?"

I brace myself, and together we pull the inert form upright.

She moans a protest, feet scrabbling for purchase, and falls against me. I draw in a sharp breath.

"Be careful, Percy. She's in the family way. And near her term, judging by the size of her."

"That's why I sent her packing. We don't want her sort round here."

Even so, he scoops the woman up, turns and carries her up the stairs, puffing with the effort. He's in his mid-forties now; the years are creeping

Illustration by Ruth Blair.

I shut the door, pick up the lantern and follow.

"I'll help you get her into bed, and light the fire," Percy says.

That word again. Twice in less than five minutes.

Such a welcome word: it implies working together, talking, loving, being together.

There's been precious little of any of that in the last three months. Not since that day in September when the biscuit-coloured envelope dropped through the letter-box.

The letter inside was pre-printed, the spaces for number, rank, name and so on filled in with black ink.

It is my painful duty to inform you . . . Private Joseph Watson . . . killed in action . . .

I remember reading the letter, then reading it a second time. I recall sinking down into a chair. I didn't cry, not then. I was too empty to cry.

Joe. My brave boy. My bright, brave boy.

Unfailingly cheerful. So willing to help; so much a presence in the house, and in the shop. I'll never see him again, or hear his voice, or feel the bristles of his moustache when he kisses my cheek.

His death has left a vast emptiness in me.

And for Percy, his enthusiasm for the shop vanished overnight.

"What's the point?" he'd said. "Who's going to take over when I die, now Joe's gone?"

Grief, I know, has left us isolated, one from the other, unable to share.

169

With a grunt, Percy lays the woman on her back in our bed. We'll decide where we'll sleep later. That day in September, we shut the door on the other bedroom, and we've never entered it since.

I hold the lantern high.

Not a woman. A girl.

She can't be more than sixteen or seventeen years old. Big with child, and begging at this time of year – it doesn't bear thinking about.

I set the lantern down on the mantelpiece and pull off my other glove. I keep my hat and coat on. It's cold in the room.

"I'll get these wet clothes off her."

I lift the girl's head and shoulders, pull the thick woollen shawl away and toss it into the corner. The girl groans, but her eyes remain closed.

Joe was nineteen back when it all started. He volunteered to fight the Kaiser, of course, like thousands of others.

How tall and upright and handsome he had looked in his khaki uniform. The cap, with the regiment's badge, made him even taller. My heart had threatened to burst with pride.

I recall my son's impatience.

"They say it's going to be over by Christmas, Mum. And I won't have even finished my training."

But it wasn't over in a few short months. It went on for four long years. It's hard to believe 1918 is now drawing to a close, and the war's been over for seven whole weeks.

"Have you seen her feet?" Percy asks, his voice sharp and anxious.

The front edges of the girl's jacket no longer meet across the swell of her stomach.

I'm busy untying the rags that have been twisted round the buttons and through each buttonhole, but I look up, and see something like horror in my husband's expression.

I reach down, pull the girl's skirts away from her feet, and suck in a shocked breath.

The girl's wearing boots, yes, but the uppers of one have parted from the sole. For the other, the girl has used pieces of bark from a tree as replacement soles, and tied them to her boots with thick ropes of rag.

I touch one with my fingertips. It's soaking wet and ice cold.

"Get them off her, Percy." My voice is gruff, and my eyes fill with tears.

Percy and I have had hard times in the past, but we've never been this poor.

"Dry them and put a pair of your socks on her. No, two pairs."

The girl moans again, legs moving restlessly.

I pull her jacket off and it joins the shawl in the corner.

Joe wrote at least once a week. Long, enthusiastic letters at first, growing shorter when he and his battalion finished their training and crossed the Channel.

He had his last home leave six months ago. I smile at the memory.

His sisters, Dorothy and Florence, were both married and in service at the manor house, but were given the afternoon off.

Percy closed the shop, and all five of us sat round the dining-room table, laughing and joking, eating white bread sandwiches and drinking tea laced with rum from the pub down the road.

But the laughter stopped, and things grew more serious later on.

Joe and I were alone in the scullery, washing the tea things.

"Mum —" he began.

My hands stilled in the hot soapy water, and I twisted my head to look at my son. There was a seriousness in his expression that tugged at my heart. He'd seen things in the war, horrible things, I was sure of it.

"Mum," he said again. "How did you know Dad was the one for you?"

I hid my surprise. It wasn't what I'd expected.

"Well, I . . . I don't know." I lifted a plate out of the water and put it to drain. "I just did."

"Did you feel sort of excited, but comfortable at the same time?"

"Well, yes, I suppose I did." I turned to look at my son again, and smiled. "Is that how you feel about Maud?"

They had announced their engagement before he left for France.

Joe paused before replying, and his thoughts seemed to be far away.

"Yes." Another pause. "Yes, I think so."

I shake my head, chasing the memories away.

"What's she doing here?" I wonder out loud, untying the strings that are holding skirt and petticoats in place. "Old Mrs Wright said she saw a beggar woman down by the coast road this morning. This must be who she saw."

There are rips in the thick green-and-black striped cloth of the skirt, and the deep frill along the lower edge has come away in places.

"How long has she been on the road, do you think?"

"Probably ever since she started to show," Percy says. "I imagine she's been thrown out of her home, or the place where she worked. No prizes for guessing why."

He nods towards the girl's left hand. No wedding ring.

"Poor child." I sigh.

The girl groans and arches her back to rub the flat of her hand down her spine. Her eyes flutter open, then close again.

I hear Percy's feet on the stairs as he runs down to fetch kindling and coal for the fire, and I pull the girl's skirt and petticoats down over her legs, leaving her in just her shift.

It's barely damp, thank goodness, but I'll change it anyway.

Then I frown and scrunch the linen petticoats in my hand. There's wetness here, but not elsewhere on the undergarments.

"Her waters have broken," I say when Percy returns.

"Can you deal with it, Grace?" He drops to his knees to set the fire.

I hesitate.

The midwife's ill with the flu, but the girl's so small and thin I feel I need someone with me.

"Get the doctor," I say. We'll worry about the expense later.

With a moan, the girl moves from side to side, her hands coming up to cup her stomach. She opens her mouth and a string of words come out.

I look helplessly at Percy.

"I caught the word 'baby', I think? But that's all."

He sits back on his heels.

"I didn't understand a thing she said."

"Could she be Welsh?" My brother's been there; he says they're difficult to understand.

Percy shrugs.

"Maybe." Reaching up to the mantelpiece, he takes the candle from the lantern and holds the flame to the twists of newspaper and slivers of wood until they catch.

"There. That should do it." Standing up, he touches my shoulder, squeezes it. "I'll go and fetch the doctor."

I catch my breath.

Affectionate gestures have been rare in recent months. But the girl's arrival has given us both something else to focus on.

I work quickly, pulling the shift up over the girl's head and replacing it with a nightdress I take from the chest of drawers.

My old one. It's likely going to get spoilt in the next few hours.

The girl moves constantly, drawing her legs up to her stomach, pushing them down, unable to remain still for long. Another stream of words comes from her lips, but I don't recognise many of them.

I wrap the quilt round her, stroke her face and murmur words of comfort and reassurance.

The tarry scent of coal fills the room. It's cosily warm, and I take off my coat and unpin my hat.

Drawing up the bedroom chair, I sit beside the girl and touch the back of my hand to her cheek. Like the room, it's much warmer now, and there's a hint of colour beneath her skin.

The girl smiles, and I find myself smiling back. Her face is heart-shaped, with large eyes and a full mouth.

Far too thin now, but with some good food inside her, she'll be pretty.

I look at the girl's hair, thick and dark in the firelight, and wonder about lice. No, I decide, I'll deal with that problem later.

And the problem of the girl herself. She can't stay here for more than a day or two. She's nothing to do with us.

Joe died near a place called Bapaume, I found out later. I'd never heard of the town before. I'd heard of Flanders, of course, but I'd had to ask the schoolteacher where Bapaume was. It's in the north of France. He showed me on the map that hangs on the wall of his schoolroom, and his kindness brought tears to my eyes.

Selfishly perhaps, I was relieved I didn't need to go round and give the news to Maud. Joe had written to his fiancée shortly after his conversation with me in the scullery, breaking off the engagement.

The girl's trying to get up, wanting to crouch or kneel on the bed. The baby's on its way.

I hear the door to the outside open and slam shut, two sets of feet on the stairs, and breathe a sigh of relief. The doctor and Percy enter the room, bringing the pungent odour of cigar smoke with them.

"It's gone midnight," the doctor says. "It'll be a Christmas baby."

Percy looks from me to the doctor to the girl, who's now kneeling on the bed, her face distorted by effort.

"I'll leave you to it."

Picking up the wet clothes from the corner, he leaves the room and goes back downstairs.

"I don't know if you'll understand her," I warn, as the doctor sets his bag on the chest of drawers. "She speaks some sort of dialect."

The doctor holds the flat of his hand to the girl's neck and pushes her gently back down on to the bed.

"I need to examine you, see how far along baby is."

His stony expression tells me he has no sympathy for the girl's condition.

She says something, her tone fast. I hear the word "baby" three times.

Frowning, the doctor turns to look at me.

"She's French. She's speaking French."

"French?" All at once there's a lump in my throat.

I cast my mind back to the map the schoolmaster had shown me. France is miles away from here. I think of the girl's boots, so worn she had to reinforce them with tree bark tied on with rags, and the realisation takes my breath away.

The girl must have walked all the way from wherever she lived in France to – where? Boulogne?

It's the only French port I know; the one where Joe and his battalion landed. She must have crossed the Channel, then walked all the miles along the coast from Dover.

Percy's feet are loud on the stairs. He bursts into the bedroom.

"I think you ought to see this. I found it in the pocket of her jacket."

It's a photo. It shows a soldier, a Tommy.

I recognise him straight away. He stands tall and stiffly upright, holding his cap under one arm, his other arm round the waist of a young woman with thick dark hair.

"It's Joe. And the girl he's with –" My voice trails away. I look at the girl on the bed, partially hidden by the bulk of the doctor's back, and my heart gives an uneasy little dance.

I hear a wail like a kitten calling, and the doctor straightens.

"It's a boy," he says. "A healthy boy."

I look at the girl. A small smile of wonder softens her face as she touches her baby's fine, dark hair.

"What's – your – name?" I ask, spacing the words out.

A babble of sound comes back in reply.

"*Espérance*," the doctor supplies. "It means 'hope'."

Hope. I can hardly believe it. Yes, there's hope now. The girl and her baby will help fill that aching void in my life.

Wordlessly, I take Percy's hand, feel him grip mine in response, drawing me to him. We're together again.

The girl smiles a shy smile as she points at her baby and says just one word. The pronunciation is a little strange but the word is unmistakable.

"Joseph." ∎

Barmouth, Gwynedd

BARMOUTH in Gwynedd, north-western Wales, is a pretty harbour located in the Mawddach Estuary. In fact, it's so pretty that when J.R.R. Tolkien visited the town, some think he made it the model for Hobbiton, the home of the hobbits, in "The Lord Of The Rings".

It's a traditional seaside town with Victorian stone villas, a lovely sandy beach, a promenade and a small fairground. There's plenty to see and do, including Tŷ Gwyn's "shipwreck museum" and Tŷ Crwn Round House, the RNLI Lifeboat Museum, and some wonderful wooded walks in the surrounding areas.

The town is overlooked by Dinas Oleu (Citadel of Light). The land used to be owned by Fanny Talbot, a local landowner and philanthropist. In 1895 she donated the land to the National Trust. It was the first property the Trust acquired in this way. ∎